Amanda Thomas · Pavla Boulton

Elevating Early Childhood Outdoor Pedagogy

Harnessing Schemas and Embracing Loose Parts

Amanda Thomas
University of South Wales
Newport, UK

Pavla Boulton
University of Gloucestershire
Gloucester, UK

ISBN 978-3-031-89782-5   ISBN 978-3-031-89783-2 (eBook)
https://doi.org/10.1007/978-3-031-89783-2

© Springer Nature Switzerland AG 2025

This work is subject to copyright. All rights are solely and exclusively licensed by the Publisher, whether the whole or part of the material is concerned, specifically the rights of translation, reprinting, reuse of illustrations, recitation, broadcasting, reproduction on microfilms or in any other physical way, and transmission or information storage and retrieval, electronic adaptation, computer software, or by similar or dissimilar methodology now known or hereafter developed.
The use of general descriptive names, registered names, trademarks, service marks, etc. in this publication does not imply, even in the absence of a specific statement, that such names are exempt from the relevant protective laws and regulations and therefore free for general use.
The publisher, the authors and the editors are safe to assume that the advice and information in this book are believed to be true and accurate at the date of publication. Neither the publisher nor the authors or the editors give a warranty, expressed or implied, with respect to the material contained herein or for any errors or omissions that may have been made. The publisher remains neutral with regard to jurisdictional claims in published maps and institutional affiliations.

Cover credit: Emily Mitchell/Alamy Stock Photo

This Palgrave Macmillan imprint is published by the registered company Springer Nature Switzerland AG
The registered company address is: Gewerbestrasse 11, 6330 Cham, Switzerland

If disposing of this product, please recycle the paper.

Elevating Early Childhood Outdoor Pedagogy

"This is a detailed, engaging and thought-provoking book full of practical and accessible ideas and information. Its effective blend of theory, practice and reflection will provide an understanding of the role schemas play in children's development and learning, making links to the unique opportunities that the outdoor environment and loose parts provide for practitioners to nurture every child's potential."

—Jane Dorrian, *Early Childhood Lecturer, The Open University, UK*

"If you have ever wondered why children display repeated patterns of behaviour in their play and exploration then this book is for you […]The importance of outdoor play and loose parts entwine beautifully with affordance theory […]It gives us permission to freely allow children to use space and objects to be whatever they want them to be."

—Claire Pudney, *Nursery Manager and Director at Meadowbank Day Nursery, Abergavenny, UK*

"This timely book is a valuable addition to supporting both students and practitioners in developing their environments so young children's schematic play can flourish. Photographs, reflective questions, case studies and further reading all help to ensure that the vital affordances for children will be considered by practitioners."

—Julie Beams, *Senior Lecturer in Education Studies at Bedfordshire University, UK*

"Supporting young children's schematic play challenges adults to be more knowledgeable and attuned to the motivations that drive young children's play. By weaving together the key themes of outdoor learning, loose parts play and schema, the book offers valuable insights into how these pedagogical approaches foster exploration, creativity, and meaningful learning experiences for young children—making it a valuable companion for anyone interested in child development."

—Julie Brierley, *Lecturer in Early Years, University of Hull, UK*

Preface

This book is intended to support and inspire Early Childhood Educators and Student practitioners in the field of early years and early childhood education, to develop knowledge and understanding of how to support children's schematic development through the use of loose parts, using the outdoor environment and nature.

It was written because early childhood experiences play such a critical role in developing a child and the three strands of nature and outdoor spaces, play and loose parts and schematic development form an intersectionality that can help to transgress teaching, bringing a holistic way of thinking to supporting young children to develop and learn.

The book hopes to foster a confidence for practitioners to take children into natural environments where children can percolate their learning at their pace, engaging with nature, and where they can connect with outdoor spaces and through that connection, nurture their schemas. It is important to have clear explanations of different dynamic schemas which are provided in this book, as well as suggestions of how to identify them and ideas for nurturing them, whilst offering case studies as examples that may help practitioners reflect on their practice and adopt new ways of thinking, that prioritise the *process* of learning not the outcome.

We hope that as you read this book, you find moments of inspiration, ideas to try, and a gentle reassurance that we work in a dynamic landscape, and so we rarely get it right first time. We hope you feel you can dip in and out of the chapters as you explore and extend your own practice and that you develop a conviction to slow down your pedagogy and to soak up the moments of learning in outdoor spaces, where children can connect with nature, helping them to make sense of the world and to develop a sense of place within it.

The authors would like to thank Helen van der Stelt, for her invaluable support with the production of this book and offering guidance and reminders along the way that we would not have thought about, to help make it into a book rather than a lot of words, pictures and ideas.

Amanda Thomas
University of South Wales
Newport, UK

Pavla Boulton
University of Gloucestershire
Gloucester, UK

Acknowledgements The authors would like to acknowledge and express their thanks to the practitioners, children and parents who participated in our research. We are grateful to have been able to observe and photograph the children's schemas, their use of loose parts and the variety of activities that took place in the enabling outdoor spaces and learning environments within the settings.

Competing Interests The authors have no competing interests to declare that are relevant to the content of this manuscript.

Contents

1	**Introduction**	1
	Why This Book is Needed	1
	Schemas	2
	Exploring the Role of Schemas in the Curriculum	3
	Outdoor Learningand Play	4
	Loose Parts	4
	Affordance Theory	5
	Overview of the Book	5
	Pause for Thought?	7
	Conclusion	7
	Opportunities for Further Reading	8
	References	8
2	**Schematic Development: A Deepening of the Dialogue**	11
	History of Schemas	11
	Jean Piaget	11
	Lev Vygotsky	13
	Chris Athey	14
	Cathy Nutbrown	15
	Cath Arnold	15
	Francis Atherton	16
	Schemas and International Research	17
	Links Between Schemas and Early Childhood Education Curricula	17
	The Importance of Observation	19
	Conclusion	22
	Reflective Questions	23
	Opportunities for Further Reading	23
	References	23

3	**Outdoor Pedagogy in Early Childhood Education**	25
	Outdoor Learning	25
	The Context of Outdoor Pedagogy	25
	Benefits of Outdoor Learning and Teaching	26
	Challenges of Outdoor Provision	28
	A Fear of the Term 'Pedagogy' Used Outdoors?	28
	Viewing Outdoor Learning as a Pedagogy to Teach the Curriculum	29
	Natural Environments Versus The Clock and the Timetable	32
	Research Spotlight	33
	Nature Pedagogy and Nature Connectedness	34
	Conclusion	35
	References	36
4	**The Ingredients of Effective Outdoor Environments and How They Can Nurture Schematic Development in Early Childhood**	39
	Research on the Benefits of Loose Parts Play (LPP)	43
	Affordance Theory	45
	How Affordance Theory Underpins Practice	46
	Effective Outdoor Environments and Schemas	47
	Where Does Risky Play Fit?	51
	Research Spotlight	52
	Conclusion	53
	References	54
5	**Rotational Schema and Loose Parts**	57
	Rotational Schema in Action	57
	Rotational Schema and Loose Parts in the Outdoors	60
	Rotational Schemas and the Four Operating Levels	60
	Curriculum Links	61
	Taking the Learning Forward	61
	Other Curricula Links-EYFS	64
	Conclusion	69
	Key Takeaways: A List of the Main Schematic Features of a Rotational Schema	70
	Opportunities for Further Reading	70
	References	70
6	**Trajectory Schema and Loose Parts**	73
	Trajectory Schema in Action	73
	Trajectory Schema and Loose Parts in the Outdoors	75
	Trajectory Schemas and the Four Operating Levels	76
	Curriculum Links	76
	Taking the Learning Forward	79

	Other Curricula Links: Realising the Ambition-Being Me in Scotland	79
	Conclusion	83
	Key Takeaways: A List of the Main Schematic Features of a Trajectory Schema	84
	Opportunities for Further Reading	84
	References	85
7	**Enclosing and Enveloping Schemas and Loose Parts**	**87**
	Enclosing and Enveloping Schema in Action	87
	Enclosing and Enveloping Schemas and Loose Parts	87
	Enclosing and Enveloping Schemas and the Four Operating Levels	90
	Curriculum Links	91
	Taking the Learning Forward	91
	Other Curricula Links: The Curriculum for Wales	94
	Conclusion	100
	Key Takeaways: A List of the Main Schematic Features of an Enclosing and Enveloping Schema	101
	Developmental Significance	102
	Opportunities for Further Reading	102
	References	102
8	**Transporting Schema and Loose Parts**	**105**
	Transporting Schema in Action	105
	Transporting Schema and Loose Parts in the Outdoors	107
	Transporting Schema and the Operating Levels	109
	Curriculum Links	110
	Taking the Learning Forward	110
	Other Curricula Links: Early Childhood Play, Learning and Care—Developmental Pathways 0–3 (Wales)	110
	Conclusion	118
	Key Takeaways: A List of the Main Schematic Features of a Transporting Schema	119
	Opportunities for Further Reading	120
	References	120
9	**Orientation and Positioning Schema and Loose Parts**	**121**
	Orientation and Positioning Schema in Action	121
	Orientation and Positioning Schemas and Loose Parts in the Outdoors	123
	Orientation and Positioning Schemas and the Four Operating Levels	123
	Curriculum Links	124
	Taking the Learning Forward	124
	Other Curricula Links-Reggio Emilia Curriculum in Italy	129
	Key Principles of the Reggio Emilia Curriculum	129

	Supporting Children's Schemas in the Reggio Emilia Approach	129
	Conclusion	134
	Key Takeaways: A List of the Main Schematic Features of an Orientation and Positioning Schema	135
	Opportunities for Further Reading	136
	References	136
10	**The Conclusion**	139
	Recapping the Structure of the Book	139
	Practical Implications for Educators and Caregivers	142
	What We Have Learnt as Authors from Writing This Book	142
	Pause for Thought Revisited	143
	References	144
References		147
Index		155

About the Authors

Dr. Amanda Thomas is a Senior Lecturer in Early Years education at USW and is joint course leader for the Early Years Education degree. She has taught in both Primary and Further Education before taking up her role in Higher Education in 2011. Amanda currently teaches on a range of education modules including play and pedagogy, child development and educational research. She completed her PhD in 2018 exploring children's schemas in the Foundation Phase in Wales. She has had books published on Early Years education and development, schemas and Transitions within education.

Pavla Boulton has been a university lecturer in Early Years Education and Practice for 15 years. She has taught across the age ranges, from primary to Further Education and has specialised in physical education and using the Forest School approach. Pavla currently teaches at the University of Gloucestershire on a range of education modules and courses, covering child development, child psychology, special educational needs and outdoor learning approaches for teaching and learning. She has published resources and papers on outdoor learning and digital technology, and schematic development in the outdoors. Pavla is currently completing her PhD which is an autoethnographic critique of mobilising early childhood educators' knowledge in Outdoor pedagogy in a time of educational reform.

Abbreviations

AoLEs	Areas of Learning and Experience
CfW	Curriculum for Wales
DfE	Department for Education
EC	Early Childhood
ECE	Early Childhood Education
ECE's	Early Childhood Educators
EY	Early Years
EYFS	Early Years Foundation Stage
IoL	Institute for Outdoor Learning
LPP	Loose Parts Play
NMCfN	Non-Maintained Curriculum for Funded Nurseries
OL	Outdoor Learning
WG	Welsh Government

List of Figures

Fig. 2.1	The observation cycle (WG, 2023a)	20
Fig. 2.2	Applying a positioning schema to the observation cycle	20
Fig. 2.3	Making a secret path	21
Fig. 3.1	Child pushing wheelbarrow: Noticing a Transporting Schema	29
Fig. 4.1	Moving a Loose part: Manoeuvring a wooden wheeled box across the yard	41
Fig. 4.2	I am hiding in my castle - An Enclosing Schema	42
Fig. 4.3	A Child pulls a wooden cart containing water jugs across the yard: A Transporting Schema	43
Fig. 4.4	Milo filling and emptying containers with soil: A Transporting schema	48
Fig. 4.5	Milo making sure all the soil it out!	49
Fig. 5.1	Twisting pipe cleaners to go through the sieve	58
Fig. 5.2	Feeling chuffed with the result	58
Fig. 5.3	Twisting the sieve down into the sand to make it come up through the holes	59
Fig. 5.4	Pouring sand into the sieve to fall through the holes	59
Fig. 5.5	Schemas in the Curriculum: Rotational Schema	62
Fig. 5.6	Rotational Schema & the five developmental pathways	63
Fig. 5.7	The observation Cycle (WG, 2023a)	66
Fig. 5.8	Using the observation cycle for Toby and Emily	67
Fig. 5.9	Rolling a hoop across the bridge	68
Fig. 6.1	George building a vertical tower indoors	74
Fig. 6.2	Ellis using loose parts to build a vertical tower outdoors	74
Fig. 6.3	Schemas in the curriculum: Trajectory schemas	77
Fig. 6.4	Trajectory schema & the five developmental pathways	78
Fig. 6.5	The observation cycle (WG, 2023a)	80
Fig. 6.6	Using the observation cycle for George and Ellis	81
Fig. 6.7	Pouring water in a downward trajectory	82
Fig. 7.1	Ross enveloped inside his outdoor enclosure	88

Fig. 7.2	Phoebe enclosing herself inside the blocks	89
Fig. 7.3	Schemas in the curriculum: Enclosing schemas	92
Fig. 7.4	Enclosing schema & the five developmental pathways	93
Fig. 7.5	Enveloping schema & the five developmental pathways	94
Fig. 7.6	Schemas in the curriculum: Enveloping schemas	95
Fig. 7.7	The observation cycle (WG, 2023a)	97
Fig. 7.8	Using the observation cycle for Ross and Phoebe	97
Fig. 7.9	Painting water inside a shape	98
Fig. 7.10	Enveloping hands inside water	99
Fig. 8.1	Transporting containers across the yard	106
Fig. 8.2	Ella transporting water from one place to another	106
Fig. 8.3	The boys have transported their goods and are now emptying them into the water tray for use	107
Fig. 8.4	Milo is transporting earth from one place to another	108
Fig. 8.5	Schemas in the curriculum: Transporting schemas	111
Fig. 8.6	Transporting schema & the five developmental pathways	112
Fig. 8.7	The observation cycle (WG, 2023a)	113
Fig. 8.8	Using the observation cycle for Milo	114
Fig. 8.9a	Charlie emptying the jugs of water into the top tray	116
Fig. 8.9b	Children transporting themselves around the yard	117
Fig. 9.1	David hangs upside down from the rope bridge	122
Fig. 9.2	On top of the pipe to be a 'tightrope' walker	122
Fig. 9.3	Schemas in the curriculum: Orientation schemas	125
Fig. 9.4	Orientation schema & the five developmental pathways	126
Fig. 9.5	Schemas in the curriculum: Positioning schemas	127
Fig. 9.6	Positioning schema & the five developmental pathways	128
Fig. 9.7	The observation cycle (WG, 2023a)	131
Fig. 9.8	Using the observation cycle for David (WG, 2023a)	131
Fig. 9.9	Positioning crates	132

List of Tables

Table 2.1	Athey's typology of action-based schemas	15
Table 4.1	An Audit of your Loose Parts and Resources	45
Table 4.2	Sandseter's Categorisation of risky play (2007)	52

Chapter 1
Introduction

Why This Book is Needed

This book has come about because of two academics wanting to deepen the dialogue and knowledge and understanding of schemas, loose parts, affordance theory and outdoor learning. This work has evolved from several projects undertaken with Early Childhood Educators (ECE's), undergraduate Early Years (EY) students, Early Childhood settings and the Welsh Government. We have developed resource materials on schemas, loose parts, affordance theory and the use of outdoors in teaching and learning for those working with young children in the early years sector. As a result of this, we have combined our knowledge of schemas and loose parts, particularly in the outdoors, and explored how this combination can afford children opportunities to wallow in their schematic endeavours.

This chapter sets the context for the rest of the book by explaining what schemas and loose parts are, and what we mean by affordance theory within the outdoors. This book is needed because from our own experiences as classroom practitioners and working with both undergraduates and postgraduate students, knowledge of schemas, loose parts and outdoor learning is patchy. This can be deemed a lost opportunity as key developmental moments can be missed and child-centred practice diminished.

This book seeks to rectify this through chapters dedicated to different action-based schemas and how to observe them, what to do once a schema has been identified, and how loose parts within an outdoor environment can and will afford children opportunities to nurture their schematic behaviour and nourish their developing cognition. It will make links to a toolkit developed by the authors that shows how different action-based schemas can be supported in the early years. This can serve as a guide

Supplementary Information The online version contains supplementary material available at https://doi.org/10.1007/978-3-031-89783-2_1.

or starting point for anyone who wants to know more about how they can recognise and support children's schemas within their practice and setting.

This book will be useful for anyone who works with young children. It will broaden knowledge and understanding of child development, the importance of loose parts and how the outdoors can be seen as full of learning potential for children and adults alike. It will be an essential book for anyone studying child development degrees and education-related degrees at both undergraduate and postgraduate level. Further students studying joint honours degrees such as psychology and education will also find this book valuable. Practitioners already working in the field of early years education will find this book beneficial particularly to refresh, reflect or engage with continuing professional development.

This introductory chapter will include a 'pause for thought' question facilitating the reader to consider their current understanding of and any questions that they may have, at this point, about schemas, loose parts and outdoor learning. This will be revisited in the conclusion chapter to ascertain if their knowledge has changed/refined/been challenged and if the initial questions have been answered. Key terminology will be defined and explained throughout the book starting with what we mean by schemas.

Schemas

There are many definitions of schemas but the one that resonated with me when I was researching schemas for my Ph.D. was from Chris Athey (1990) who stated that schemas were, 'a pattern of repeatable behaviour into which experiences are assimilated and that are gradually co-ordinated' (p. 37). Children will repeatedly use action-based schemas facilitated by objects in their environment to develop their knowledge and understanding of their world. Reflecting upon my time in the classroom, I can certainly remember children who seemed to carry out repeated patterns of behaviour in their play, which I observed but did not explore further or plan for.

However, other definitions are as follows starting with Piaget. Schema is the label Piaget gave to cognitive structures that individuals use to internalise their actions. Piaget held that, 'thought consists of internalised and co-ordinated action schemas' (Piaget 1959, pp. 357–86). For Piaget, the function of a schema was to allow generalisations to be made about objects and events in the environment where the schema was being applied (Piaget 1970). Piaget stated that, 'Schemas of action [are] co-ordinated systems of movements and perceptions, which constitute any elemental behaviour capable of being repeated and applied to new situations, e.g. *grasping, moving, shaking* an object' (Piaget 1962, p. 274). Neisser offered the following definition of schemas, 'as a pattern of action as well as a pattern for action' (Neisser, 1976, p. 56). Gardner (1984, p. 64) supported Neisser's definition of the active nature of schemas by stating that 'Individuals bring schemas to bear on objects in the environment... the child is involved in knowledge construction'. Meltzoff and Moore (1998, p. 229) agreed that schemas are 'initial mental structures' that 'serve as discovery procedures', again echoing the active nature of schemas. McVee et al. (2005) also supported the notion of schemas as being active, organising features that the mind imposes on experiences but also as a 'mental representation that mediates activity' (p. 550). Then more recently, Nutbrown's definition of schemas is a 'pattern of behaviour which has a consistent thread running through it' (2006, p. 10). Finally, for Louis et al. (2008) schemas are defined as, 'The word 'schema' is generally used to describe patterns of repeated behaviour which children use to explore and express their developing ideas and thoughts through play and exploration' (p. 11).

Exploring the Role of Schemas in the Curriculum

Research carried out by Arnold et al. (2010), Nutbrown (2006), Atherton and Nutbrown (2013) and Constable (2013) has shown how schemas can be embedded into the English, Early Years Foundation Stage (EYFS). Here, through detailed observations of children during play activities, the researchers were able to note children's preferred schemas and to support them with appropriate resources that nourished their forms of thought and supported their development of curriculum concepts. By following and supporting these threads of thinking, the researchers noted how the children used their schemas during play to solve problems and gain information about the world around them. This reinforces the importance of play-based provision for young children, where children can problem solve and try out ideas in an environment with supportive practitioners. As Smidt (2011) states a child engaging in play will be exploring the world, people and the objects within it. As Bruce, Louis and McCall (2015, p. 77) state, 'Knowing about schemas gives practitioners a framework through which to interpret their observations. In the policy guidance on the EYFS there are many references to active learning, play and exploration, creativity and critical thinking, all key concepts that equally apply to the development of schemas (Louis et al., 2008; DFE, 2024). Each of the chapters on specific schemas will explore that schema through a specific curriculum lens. This will show how schemas can be supported throughout early years curricula.

Previous studies into children's schemas have used detailed observations of the children at play to discover their schemas. Researchers have then nurtured and nourished these schemas through the provision of resources and activities. Palaiologou (2016) highlights the importance of observation for identifying children's interests and skills and that observations should be at the centre of practitioner practice. Throughout the chapter on specific schemas, there will be an example of how an observation cycle can be used to support children's schemas.

Outdoor Learning and Play

The values and importance of outdoor learning and play particularly in early childhood education are and have been demonstrated and researched by pioneers such as Macmillan, Montessori, Steiner and Froebel (Tovey, 2007). The importance of the outdoor environment as a 'classroom' was championed by these pioneers because of its potential to foster children's independence, encouraging active learning, experiential opportunities, contact with nature and the outdoors and opportunities to support all aspects of child development (Constable, 2015).

Outdoor learning can be defined as a planned learning activity, which may be connected to curriculum outcomes and that may be organised within the confines of the school environment and beyond, including playful encounters with materials, objects and equipment. Outdoor learning and play allows children to develop physical coordination, balance and control; it can be made up of small but significant experiences that afford children 'everyday adventures'. It provides unpredictable but essential elements of growing up, of making judgements about their physical abilities, taking risks as well as making friends. But these elements depend on being 'out and about' and not being closeted indoors (Gill, 2007).

The benefits of learning and playing in the outdoors are well documented and suggest that the outdoor environment engages children in deep learning and supports physical, cognitive, social and emotional aspects of their development (Bilton & Waters, 2016; Brussoni et al., 2015).

Loose Parts

The theory of 'loose parts' was proposed by architect, Simon Nicholson (1972). He described them as 'variables' and included things like materials, smells, gases, fluids and music, animals and plants all of which he declared children loved to play with and experiment, becoming 'inventors'. Nicholson proposed that loose parts were 'all the things that satisfy one's curiosity and give us the pleasure that results from discovery and invention' (1972, p. 30). Loose parts are resources that facilitate open-ended play and can support children's holistic development. Objects like buckets, drainpipes, tyres, jugs, wheeled toys, pebbles, sticks, logs, blocks, blankets and many more, provide rich opportunities for children to problem solve and make sense of their world. In the outdoors, loose parts are generally larger and messier, and the space encourages children to manoeuvre objects in ways that are not possible indoors, offering better play experiences (Casey and Robertson, 2017).

Affordance Theory

American psychologist James Gibson (1979) suggested that environments and objects within them have values and meanings that are unique to the person perceiving them. The 'affordances' of an object or space are all the things it has the 'potential to do or be'. When children play in a space or with an object, they experience it in a unique way. Rather than its intended purpose, they may view it in terms of its 'affordances'. For example, a drainpipe might be considered for collecting water, but for a child it might be used to transport a ball or a toy car from one point to another. Different objects have different affordances, and so children can learn more deeply as they engage with the same concept using different objects, engaging the senses in a multi-faceted way, thus affording opportunities for children to nurture their schemas.

Overview of the Book

Chapter Two: Schematic Development—A Deepening of the Dialogue—gives the history of schemas, what they are, theories linked to schemas, schema types, links to various curricula, observations in practice and informing planning. This chapter will provide a history of schemas, starting with the work of Piaget and moving on to contemporary authors who have taken his work on schemas forward, such as Chris Athey, Cathy Nutbrown and Cath Arnold. It will look at how schemas can support child development and knowledge construction. Athey's work will be explored in terms of her naming of action-based dynamic schemas and how they can be observed in practice. Links will be made to several EY curricula and how a knowledge and understanding of schemas can support different areas of learning and experience and developmental pathways. This chapter will discuss the importance of observations in noting schemas and how, once noted, adults can provide effective, enabling learning environments and engaging learning experiences. Within this chapter, there will be links to online resources that can support readers in understanding schemas. There will be case studies and reflective questions included throughout the chapter along with an end of chapter summary, questions, opportunities for further reading and a chapter reference list.

Chapter Three: Outdoor Pedagogy in Early Childhood Education—will explore outdoor pedagogy in the EY with a background to outdoor learning and the importance of outdoor learning and play in the EY. It will consider the benefits and challenges to provision through the curriculum and of outdoor learning pedagogy and play. This chapter will look at how the outdoors supports areas of development including cognitive development, risky play and its role in developing self-awareness and self-regulation. Outdoor pedagogy can play a role in nurturing children's schemas. This chapter will provide case studies/photographs/ and an opportunity for an audit of your own outdoor provision. There will be opportunities for further reading and a chapter reference list.

Chapter Four: The Ingredients of Effective Outdoor Environments—offers some background theory to support the pedagogical tools addressed in the chapter. It will explain the theory of loose parts and what they are, how they can be used in the outdoors, how they magnify opportunities for children's development, and offer opportunities for collaboration and democracy in children's play (Hobson, 2020). An explanation of affordance theory (Gibson 1979) is also discussed; why is it important for practitioners to understand affordance theory and how it affects planning and provision. There will be a task included to encourage practitioners to audit the loose parts in their setting and to evaluate their use, effectiveness and level of curiosity that they instigate with the children—a template to conduct the audit is provided as well. Affordance theory helps us to see the world from a child's unique perspective and understand that every child will see a value in a resource that others do not see. This can underpin patterns of behaviour that can help us to explore schemas in children's development.

Chapters 5–9: Chapters on Different Schematic Types—Schema Types covered: Rotational, Trajectory, Enclosing & enveloping, Transporting, Orientation and Positioning. The chapters will give a definition of what each schema is, and each chapter will have several annotated photos of children evidencing the dynamic aspect of each schema in the outdoors using loose parts. There are case studies discussing what has been seen in practice, linked to reflective questions. These chapters include links to theory around schemas, loose parts and outdoor pedagogy (supporting the work written in Chapters 2, 3 and 4).

Each of Chapters 5–9 will make a link to a schematic toolkit produced by the authors for the Curriculum for Funded Non-maintained Nursery Settings (Boulton & Thomas, 2023). This online schema toolkit offers guidance on resources (including a range of loose parts), and what activities provide opportunities to nurture different schemas. It will show what supportive language adults can use to nourish a child's action-based schema, and how to plan the next steps.

You can use this hyperlink to take you to the Schematic Development Toolkit (Boulton & Thomas, 2023).

https://hwb.gov.wales/repository/resource/39397e24-d5e9-4b57-ad15-09f64f4ad0ec/overview

This will be referred to throughout our book.

In addition to this link to the toolkit, there will be links made to different curricula within the different chapters and areas of learning and experience showing how schemas can support knowledge generation throughout EY curricula. The observation cycle will be shown in each chapter, and how it can be used by practitioners to recognise and support different schematic behaviours. There will be case studies, followed by questions and a chapter conclusion. There will be reflective questions for the reader to consider linked to the chapter and a recommend further reading.

Chapter 10. The Conclusion—drawing out the key messages, summarising implications for practice and then returning to the 'pause for thought' questions posed in the introduction. This chapter will recap and reflect upon the previous chapters, and it will reflect upon the key messages interwoven throughout the book. There will be a section on what we, as the authors, have learned from writing the book and there will be several questions asking the reader what they have learned from reading the book. The reader will be asked to return to their initial understanding of outdoor pedagogies and schemas, and any questions they may have had in the 'pause for thought' section of the introductory chapter. The reader can consider whether their questions have been answered having read the book and if their initial understanding has changed and how it has changed. Readers will be asked about at least one thing they will take from this book and try out in practice. This chapter will again provide links to access the complete Schematic development teaching toolkit which readers can access as a downloadable pdf—free of charge. Following this chapter, there will be a full glossary and reference list.

Pause for Thought?

- What do you think is most relevant for you to know about schemas, loose parts and outdoor learning?

You will have an opportunity to revisit this question in the concluding chapter. We hope that by the time you get to the conclusion you will have a deeper understanding of schemas, loose parts and outdoor learning. We hope that your knowledge will have changed/improved/been refined/and been challenged from reading the book.

Conclusion

This opening chapter has given you a flavour of what this book is about. It has introduced schemas, loose parts, outdoor learning and play, and affordance theory. These will be explored in greater detail throughout the book. By engaging with the case studies and reflective questions within the chapters, there is the opportunity for the reader to deepen their knowledge and understanding and consider their own practice. This book seeks to facilitate a better and richer understanding of children's development and the different ways they construct their knowledge and understanding.

Opportunities for Further Reading

- Boulton, P., & Thomas, A. (2023). *Schemas, outdoor play and Froebel.* Available via: https://www.froebel.org.uk/news/schemas-outdoor-play-and-froebel. Accessed Dec 23 2024.
- Grimmer, T. (2017). *Observing and developing schematic behaviour in young children: A professional's guide for supporting children's learning, play and development.* London: Jessica Kingsley Publishers.
- Clark, A. (2023). *Slow knowledge and the unhurried child.* Oxon: Routledge.

References

Arnold, C., The Pen Green Team. (2010). *Understanding schemas and emotion.* London: SAGE.
Atherton, F., & Nutbrown, C. (2013). *Understanding schemas and young children.* London: SAGE.
Athey, C. (1990). *Extending thought in young children: A parent–teacher partnership.* London: Paul Chapman.
Bilton, H., & Waters, J. (2016). Why take young children outside? A critical consideration of the professed aims for outdoor learning in the early years by teachers from England and wales. *Journal of Social Sciences.* https://doi.org/10.3390/socsci6010001
Bruce, T., Louis, S., & McCall, H. (2015). *Observing young children.* London: SAGE.
Brussoni, M., Gibbons, R., Casey, G., Ishikawa, T., Sandseter, E., Bienenstock, A., Chabot, G., Fuselli, P., Herrington, S., Janssen, I., Pickett, W., Power, M., Stanger, N., Sampson, M., & Tremblay, M. S. (2015). What is the relationship between risky outdoor play and health in children? A systematic review. *International Journal of Environmental Research and Public Health, 12,* 6423–6454.
Casey, T. and Robertson, J. (2017). *Resources for Playing - providing loose parts to support children's play.* Play Wales: Cardiff.
Constable, K. (2013). *Planning for schematic learning in the early years.* Oxon: Routledge.
Constable, K. (2015). *The Outdoor Classroom in Practice: Ages 3–7. A Month-by-Month Guide to Forest School Provision.* Routledge: London.
DFE. (2024). *Early years foundation stage statutory framework for group and school-based providers.* Available via: https://www.gov.uk/government/publications/early-years-foundation-stage-framework--2. Accessed 14 October 2024.
Gardner, H. (1984). *Frames of mind: The theory of multiple intelligences.* London: Heinemann.
Gibson, J. J. (1979). *The ecological approach to visual perception.* Mifflin: Houghton.
Gill, T. (2007). *No Fear: Growing up in a Risk Averse Society.* Calouste Galbenkian Foundation: London.
Hobson, T. (2020). *Integrating Loose Parts Play in a Preschool Program.* Available online at: https://www.edutopia.org/article/integrating-loose-parts-play-preschool-program/ (Retrieved September 2025).
Louis, S., Beswick, C., Magraw, L., Hayes, L., & Featherstone, S. (2008). *Again, again, understanding schemas in young children.* London: Black.
McVee, M., Dunsmore, K., & Gavelek, J. (2005). Schema theory revisited. *Review of Educational Research, 75*(4), 531–566.
Meltzoff, A., & Moore, M. (1998). Object representation, identity, and the paradox of early permanence: Steps toward a new framework. *Infant Behaviour and Development, 21*(2), 201–235.
Neisser, U. (1976). *Cognition and reality.* San Francisco: W. H. Freeman.

References

Nicholson, S. (1972). The theory of loose parts, an important principle for design methodology. *Studies in Design Education Craft and Technology, 4*(2), 1.
Nutbrown, C. (2006). *Key concepts in early childhood education and care*. London: SAGE.
Palaiologou, I. (2016). *Child observation* (3rd ed.). London: SAGE.
Piaget, J. (1959). *The language and thought of the child*. London: Routledge and Kegan Paul.
Piaget, J. (1962). *Play, dreams and imitation in childhood*. London: Routledge and Kegan Paul.
Piaget, J. (1970). *Science of education and the psychology of the child*. Harlow: Longman.
Smidt, S. (2011). *Playing to Learn: The role of play in the early years*. London: Routledge.
Tovey, H. (2007). *Playing Outdoors: Spaces and Places, Risk and Challenge*. McGraw: UK.

Chapter 2
Schematic Development: A Deepening of the Dialogue

Definition There are numerous definitions of schemas but as stated in chapter one, the definition that resonates with my work on schemas is from Chris Athey (1990), 'a pattern of repeatable behaviour into which experiences are assimilated and that are gradually co-ordinated' (p. 37).

History of Schemas

Jean Piaget

Jean Piaget is recognised for introducing schemas within a structured developmental framework and he has been hugely influential in the study of child development. He believed that knowledge must be invented or constructed by each learner through their actions (Piaget 1972). Piaget argued against children being told knowledge, but to find it out for themselves, through active explorations (1972). Piaget's theory of how children actively construct their knowledge and understanding was as follows:

- Assimilation—the integration of new knowledge and understanding into existing ideas.
- Accommodation—where assimilated knowledge is differentiated according to new experiences

(Piaget 1972)

Piaget argued that children and adults needed to adjust their thinking continually, in terms of new ideas and acquired knowledge. He believed that nature and nurture contributed to intellectual ability and stressed that children needed to be active learners (Piaget 1972; Maynard & Thomas, 2009). Piaget suggested that children organise their knowledge and understanding of the world into cognitive structures called schemas (1953, 1959, 1970). He believed that children learn through repeated actions and behaviours on objects and materials within their environment and through these repeated actions, working theories are built up and developed. Any new experiences are fitted into the existing schema (assimilation) so that equilibrium is maintained or if the experience is new or different, then the child alters (adapts) their schema to accommodate this new experience. In this way, new thinking and knowledge are constructed and cognitive gains are made.

Piaget (1973) was interested in the sequence of cognitive development and how children developed their understanding of the world. He proposed four stages of cognitive development which represented children's thoughts. This is known as the Stage Level Theory and he regarded development as discontinuous in as much as the children need to proceed through the four stages without missing any of the stages out or returning to them, i.e. the stages were invariant. The four stages are defined as follows: The sensori-motor stage, approximately 0–18 months; the pre-operational stage, approximately 18 months–7 years; the concrete operational stage, approximately 7 years–12 years and the formal operational stage, approximately 12 years-adulthood.

In the sensori-motor stage, the infant is seen to develop their cognition through their senses and active exploration (Piaget & Inhelder, 1969). The next stage—the pre-operation stage represents children aged 18 months–7 years. In this stage, a child's cognition continues to develop and children increasingly engage in imaginative, symbolic play and pretend play. When young children re-present their earlier experiences, they often use 'symbols' to signify or to stand for the objects, people or events they are re-enacting. These symbols can be actions, objects, pictures or words. Piaget (1972) cited observations of his own daughter engaging in imaginative play representing this stage of development and thinking. This stage is sub divided into the following two substages: *Symbolic function* and *Intuitive thought.* Within the first of these substages (2–4 years), the infant increasingly uses symbols such as images, words and gestures to represent objects. Additionally, within this substage children are egocentric, only seeing things from their point of view (Halpenny & Pettersen, 2014).

In the second substage, *Intuitive thought*, children begin to be able to search for logical explanations, begin to classify objects but have difficulty in arranging things in order (seriation) and to understand conservation. The child in the pre-operation stage continues to initiate activities where they can explore and expand their thinking and can use their preferred schemas to facilitate this.

The concrete operational stage signposts the development of logical thought in children aged 7–11 years. Here children can conserve numbers and quantities and reverse their thoughts when problem solving (Piaget 1969). The final stage in Piaget's theory of development is the formal operations stage, beginning at about 11 years of age. Here thinking is more flexible without the need for concrete props and more symbolic. However, Sunderland points out that Piaget failed to fully describe this last stage (1992). The lack of a full description of this last stage may be because Piaget did not believe that development ended once the formal operations stage was reached; he held the belief that development never ends (Piaget 1973).

Piaget (1962) contended that schemas function within the four stages detailed above and Chris Athey (1990, 2007) exemplified these stages in her research. During all these four developmental stages, the child interacts with the environment, building upon their cognitive structures. As stated previously in this chapter, if the new experiences a child is having fit into their cognitive structures, then the child maintains equilibrium. However, if the experience is new the child needs to alter their thinking and cognitive structures to accommodate these new ideas. Piaget termed this Stage Level Theory, and it relates to the four developmental stages detailed above (Louis et al., 2008).

The four stages are as follows. Schemas functioning in an active way are called sensory-motor explorations. Here a schema is demonstrated through repeated actions such as a rotational schema being seen through children twirling a hoop, drawing, or painting circles and constructing spirals or coils out of playdough. When children begin to use objects to represent something else (symbolically), this is called symbolic representation. Symbolic representations use 'actions, mark making and other graphic forms and speech (Athey, 2013, p. 9)'. An example would be children using an enveloping schema to climb inside a box which they call a *castle*.

When schemas are operating at the functional dependency level, the relationship is based on actions and their effects, so a child with a trajectory schema will discover to ride a bicycle from A to B, the pedals need to be turned to make the bike move. The final stage that schema operates at is termed the development of thought. This is when children can recall and represent events about people and objects without needing recourse to a concrete reminder. An example is a child with an enclosing schema bandaging a toy dog whilst talking about a trip to the vet (Thomas, 2018b).

However, it is important to note that children do not function at one schematic level or stage but move in and out of them in accordance with their developing intellectual capabilities at any given time (Bruce, 2011). Athey (2013) argued against thinking of these stages as hierarchical but more as interacting depending on the activity a person is engaged in. She stated that the four levels or stages in which schemas manifest themselves can be thought of 'as a progression in 'coming to know'' (p. 9). Piaget's work on schemas has provided a basis for understanding child development. By identifying children's schemas, educators can provide learning experiences attuned to their patterns of interest, develop their threads of thinking and therefore provide consistency of learning opportunities (Nutbrown 2011).

Lev Vygotsky

Although both Piaget and Vygotsky were termed constructivists, Vygotsky emphasised the belief that children learn from being part of a social environment and was known as a social constructivist. Vygotsky's work was undertaken at the same time as Piaget's work but differs in that Vygotsky believed that society and culture played a part in a child development and learning (England, 2018). Vygotsky emphasised the need for more knowledgeable others to support children and to accelerate their learning (Vygotsky 1978). He introduced the concept of scaffolding a child's learning through the zone of proximal development (ZPD).

Similar to Piaget, Vygotsky also felt that young children learn by first hand experiences and build upon previous experiences (Meade & Cubey, 2008). In terms of schemas both theories can be used as follows: Piaget's theory facilitates practitioners in understanding and recognising children's schemas and how children's cognition develops. Vygotsky's theory can be used to scaffold children's learning in terms of their preferred schemas by adding resources and using appropriate language in the learning environment.

Chris Athey

As stated previously, Athey built upon Piaget's work in the 1970s and published her findings in her book, 'Extending Thought in Young Children' (1990). Here she defined schemas as, 'a pattern or repeatable behaviour into which experiences are assimilated and that are gradually co-ordinated' (1990, p. 37). Whilst Piaget was the first to identify schemas, Athey was the first to pioneer observations of schemas (Athey 1990, 2007). She worked with Tina Bruce and analysed observations using Piaget's different schema levels or stages to make a detailed study of how young children acquire knowledge. The aim of this research was to look for schemas in a nursery setting. Athey worked with children aged 2–5 years over a 2-year period, carrying out more than five thousand observations (Athey 1990, 2007). By observing children at play, Athey was able to make a detailed study of how young children acquire knowledge and how their schemas supported this. Athey shared her observations with parents, and they reciprocated by sharing their own observations of examples of children's schemas at home. Athey reported that 'Ongoing analysis of observations made daily during the project provided the main substance of communication with parents' (1990, p. 51). The observations were interpreted using Piaget's notion of schemas and the project revealed links between speech, comprehension and prominent schemas. Athey (1990, 2007) named specific dynamic schemas emerging from action in her research as shown in the table.

In addition to the dynamic, action-based schemas shown in Table 2.1, there are positioning, connecting and disconnecting schemas. Athey also identified graphic schemas and space schemas (2007). Whilst it is important to acknowledge that schemas can also be seen through mark-making, the focus of this book is dynamic action-based schemas and how loose parts can support children's schemas, especially in the outdoors.

History of Schemas

Table 2.1 Athey's typology of action-based schemas

Dynamic vertical	
Dynamic back and forth	
Circular direction and rotation	
Going over, under or on top of	
Going round a boundary	
Enveloping and containing	
Going through boundary	

Cathy Nutbrown

Cathy Nutbrown's research (2006, 2011) discovered links between children's schemas and their talk, action, representations and thinking. Nutbrown (2011, p. 46) defined schemas as, 'threads of thinking' and schemas to be at the 'core of children's developing minds'. She built on the work of Piaget, Vygotsky, Athey and Bruce and collected observations in an early years' setting over a 10-year period. Through these observations, she made links between children's schemas and their developing understanding of maths, science and literacy (Nutbrown, 2006, 2011). Like Athey, Nutbrown argued for the process of learning or *coming to know* as more important than the end product (2011).

In Nutbrown's research regarding mathematics, 'three major schemas emerged…- dynamic vertical, dynamic circular and enveloping/containing and with each schema, one idea appeared to dominate…'

- Dynamic vertical—children were involved in activities to do with height
- Dynamic circular—children were exploring aspects of rotation and roundness
- Containing/enveloping—instances to do with capacity were observed

(Nutbrown, 2006, p. 60)

Nutbrown has also drawn attention to the importance of stories as a means of nourishing children's schemas, making links between children's preferred schemas and different stories. She has stressed that stories are a 'key source of learning material in the early years' with 'many books foster*ing* more than one schema' (2011, p. 128). In keeping with other studies into schemas, Nutbrown, (2006, 2011) also used naturalistic observations as a tool to identify children's schemas.

Cath Arnold

Cath Arnold and the team at Pen Green in Corby have explored the link between schemas and emotions (Arnold et al., 2010). Arnold discussed individual case studies of children and through observations, linked their schemas to their emotional well-being. She proposed that children's schemas and emotional events in their lives were closely linked. Arnold drew links between 'schemas explored and emotions experienced' but did accept that schemas were not necessarily prompted by emotions' (2010, p. 11). This is in contrast to the work of Nutbrown who explores schemas through a cognitive lens, whereas Arnold explores schemas through their connections with social and emotional development.

Another area of Arnold and the Pen Green team's research has been to present observations of young children's schemas in detail but to then also revisit these children in later life. What has been interesting is when revisting these children, they remember their time at Pen Green but also still seem to have interests that still reflect their orginally observed schemas. An example is Jack whose schema interests were trajectories and connections (Prodger, 2013). Whilst at Pen Green, Jack constructed a number of models including an umbrella out of construction materials, when the team revisited him at age eleven, Jack's interests still included making models albeit more complex versions than an umbrella. This illuminates what Bruce meant when she argued that, schemas do not disappear in later life but become more complex and sophisticated (2011).

Arnold's most recent work on schemas can be found in the book, 'Schemas in the Early Years' published in 2023 with the Pen Green Schema group. This book is written by academic researchers including myself, and professionals who are passionate about schemas. It explores schemas and language; schemas and movement and schematic play with autistic children, to name just a few of the chapters.

Francis Atherton

Atherton has published work with Nutbrown on schemas with children aged from birth to three (2013). Here, Atherton observed seven children over 18 months in a day care setting and the role of the adult and the learning environment were noted. Photographs of the children, 'at play highlighted consistent patterns in children's actions, speech and representations' (Atherton and Nutbrown 2013, p. X). Parents were invited to share their stories of their children's schematic behaviours at home and parents were positive about coming to understand their children's behaviours through schemas. The observations of the children's schemas were linked to the schema levels postulated by Piaget and put into practice by Athey (2007). Atherton also discussed the importance of the role of the adult in accompanying children in the learning environment through, 'attuned, matched learning encounters' (2013, p. X). As Atherton (2013) asserts, the real significance of schemas is for practice, with a knowledge of schemas allowing practitioners to understand *how* children learn. Knowing about a child's schema allows practitioners to tune into children's forms of thinking and their unique ways of *comingto know* (Atherton and Nutbrown 2013).

Schemas and International Research

Meade and Cubey carried out two studies into children's schemas in New Zealand in 1993 and between 2003 and 2006 within the Te Whāriki curriculum. The findings from this research indicated that children attending the settings, which were promoting learning through schemas, had more positive dispositions to learning. The first study focused on nine children aged between 4 and 5 years of age focusing on their mathematical and science-related schemas. This was an action research study where the teachers and researchers were developing, 'new understandings of pedagogy' (Meade & Cubey, 2008, p. 15). The data were collected through observations of the nine children to determine their dominant schemas and parents were also asked to keep records of schemas seen at home through observations. In addition, another eight children were chosen as comparison subjects, giving a total sample size of seventeen children. Nine learning competencies were assessed and compared in all children. The competencies were placed into two categories: *Being* and *Doing* (Meade & Cubey, 2008). The four *Being* competences were: social-emotional; communication, exploration and intrapersonal. These competencies were measured using observation, assessments and interviews with 'significant' adults in the child's life. The five *Doing* competences were about what the children could do. These were social problem solving, early literacy, early mathematics, logical reasoning and motor skills. These were assessed by means of an interview with the children.

Overall, the outcomes for the children in the schema setting were higher than in the comparison centre, with the results seeming to be linked with the 'schema children having more interactions and opportunities to explore' (Meade & Cubey, 2008, p. 86). However, the sample size was small so Meade and Cubey stipulated that explanations that schema children showed better scores could only be speculative (2008).

In a second in-depth case study of six children carried out by Meade and Cubey (2008), it was found that children's dispositions of concentration, persistence and involvement were stronger when their schematic interests were supported. Here the adults viewed the children as, 'active and competent learners' (Meade & Cubey, 2008, p. 127). This positive view of the child supported dispositions to learning in science, mathematics and literacy.

Question

- Which of the authors' works detailed above resonates with you and which would you like to explore in more detail?

Links Between Schemas and Early Childhood Education Curricula

Some of the researchers detailed in this chapter have carried out their work on schemas within the context of early childhood education curricula. Atherton has made links between her observations of children and the Early Years Foundation Stage

(EYFS) curriculum (Atherton and Nutbrown 2013) and Karen Constable (2013) also researched work on schemas in the EYFS. She observed children's schemas in a school setting with children aged 4–5 years and made links to the Early Years Foundation Stage (EYFS). She has shown how children's learning can be taken forward within the EYFS curriculum by supporting their schemas. Constable has given examples of how children's different schemas can be supported in a busy school setting under common early years themes or topics, and she has provided evidence of how children have taken their own learning forward using their preferred schemas. An example cited by Constable is a child with an enveloping and containing schema who can be given opportunities to build a den outdoors with others. Here the child has achieved the early learning goals for 30–50 months, 'Children can play in a group, extending and elaborating play ideas' (2013, p. 71) whilst also being supported in their enveloping and containing schemas. In terms of schemas within the current EYFS curriculum documents, there is no mention specifically of the term schema. However, in the 2012 version of the curriculum schemas were mentioned and were an intrinsic part of child development, and that practitioners should 'encourage independence as young children explore patterns of movement, sometimes referred to as schemas' (Louis 2016).

Links between children's schemas and the then Foundation Phase (FP) curriculum in Wales for children aged 3–7 years have been made through research undertaken by the authors. Thomas (2018a, 2018b) has explored several dynamic action schemas and how they can be nurtured and nourished within the FP. This research was undertaken with staff within an early years' setting and led to a toolkit published on the Welsh Government (WG) website showing how schemas could be supported in the FP and the proposed Curriculum for Wales (Thomas, 2018a). Further research on schemas and loose parts especially in the outdoors was undertaken by the authors within a nursery setting in Wales and published in 2022 (Boulton & Thomas, 2022a). This research has shown how loose parts afford children the opportunities to explore their schemas on a large scale and this will be explored throughout the book in more detail.

In 2022 Wales produced a curriculum for funded non-maintained settings; within this curriculum schemas are introduced on page 38. Here it explores how schemas can support children's development through play and how schemas can lay the foundations for 'future mathematical and scientific understanding' (WG, 2022a, p. 38). There are five developmental pathways in this curriculum as follows: belonging, communication, exploration, physical development and wellbeing. A child's schema can be linked to each of these pathways as supporting their schema gives them a sense of belonging, it enhances their wellbeing, they are eager to communicate what they are doing, and they are using their physical development and exploring through their schematic behaviours.

Different types of action-based schemas are named and there are reflective questions to allow the reader to consider their own practice. More recent research into schemas within the early childhood education curricula in Wales has led to the development of a toolkit for non-maintained settings which is also available on the WG website (Boulton & Thomas 2022b). This toolkit will be referred to in the following chapters within this book which are based on specific schemas. The toolkit has also been supported by a suite of resources produced by academics for the Welsh Government on schematic development covering child development, schematic development and effective environments (WG, 2022b).

The non-maintained curriculum also discusses the importance of the three E's which are: enabling adults, engaging experiences and effective environments. To support and nurture children's schemas, all three of these are needed. Children need attuned adults who can observe children's fascinations and ways of learning in an effective environment that has lots of engaging experiences to nurture and nourish children's schemas (WG, 2022a).

In comparison, the Curriculum for Wales (CfW) (WG, 2020b) for 3- to 16-year-olds, which became mandatory in September 2022 for all children in primary schools and is being rolled out for all learners up to sixteen by 2026, does not mention schemas. This is disappointing as some settings are using this curriculum with their 3-year-olds and this could mean a child coming from a non-maintained setting where their schemas have been supported, into a setting at the age of three or four where schemas are not known about or supported.

In Scotland, there is a curriculum from early years through to primary school called 'Realising the Ambition—Being Me' (Education Scotland, 2020). Within this document, there is a section on schemas and how to spot them and support them for early childhood education practitioners. This also includes a section on supporting parents in recognising schemas with downloadable resources and video clips (see: https://education.gov.scot/parentzone/learning-at-home/schemas/).

Different Early Years curricula will be explored in the chapters on specific schemas, showing how schemas can be supported by these curricula, thus echoing what Cathy Nutbrown espoused when she stated, 'Children's ways of learning do not change because national policies or the prescribed curriculum change' (2011, p. 128).

The Importance of Observation

As the definition states, schemas are 'repeated patterns of behaviour' (Athey 1990) that are noted through careful observation. All early childhood education curricula state the importance of careful observation with young children. Through observation repeated play behaviours and patterns can be noted and reflected upon, allowing practitioners to develop child-centred pedagogies. The observation cycle shown in Fig. 2.1 illustrates how noticing what a child does leads to analysing their behaviour and then responding with appropriate activities, resources and vocabulary.

An example of this cycle in practice would be as follows for a child with a positioning schema (Fig. 2.2):

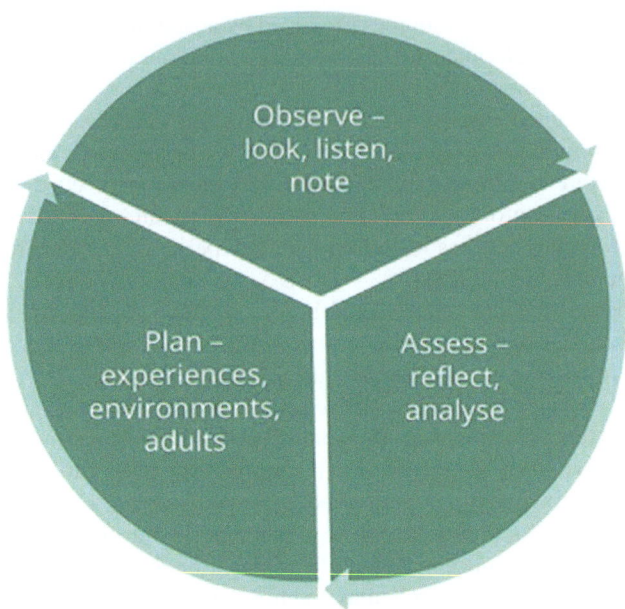

Fig. 2.1 The observation cycle (WG, 2023a)[1]

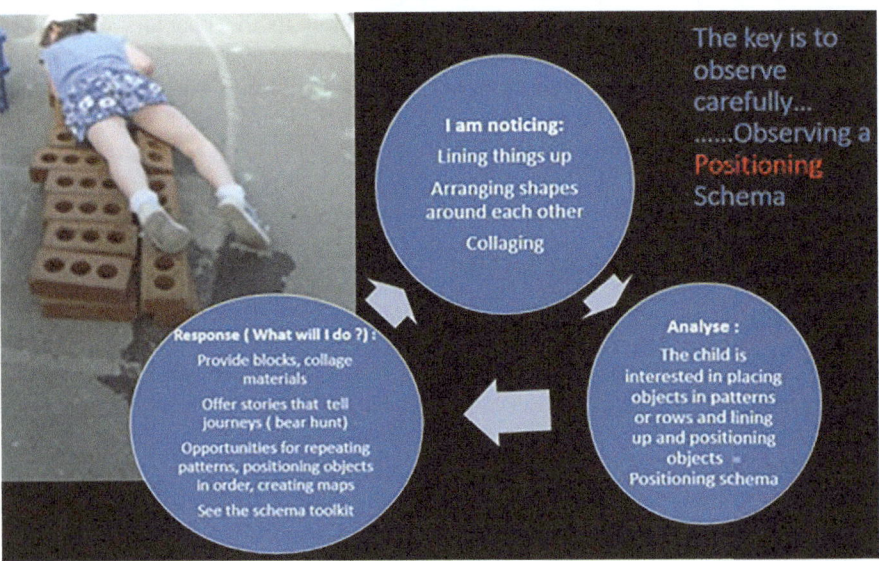

Fig. 2.2 Applying a positioning schema to the observation cycle

---

[1] View-Hwb (gov.wales).

Through careful and repeated observations, the practitioners in the setting have noted that this child has repeatedly positioned objects. In this case, she was positioning bricks to make 'her bed'. Each time she was outdoors, she worked with the bricks (loose parts) to position them to make a bed of the right length and width. On another occasion, she positioned wooden blocks to make a rectangular outline and when asked said it was a 'secret' path (Fig. 2.3).

It is important to note that some children have dominant schemas for a period of time and then move on to a different dominant schema, whilst others have a mixture of schemas and some children do not show schematic behaviour at all, but the key to noticing and providing for schemas is observation.

Practitioners in the setting used written observations and snapshot observations to note this child's play patterns and how she used the resources both indoors and outdoors to nourish and nurture her positioning schema. They ensured that there were resources available (by referring to the toolkit-Boulton & Thomas, 2022b) which allowed the child to explore her positioning schema both indoors and outdoors.

Fig. 2.3 Making a secret path

Case Study: Meadowrush Nursery is a busy setting with an enclosed outdoor area. David has been at the nursery for several weeks and his keyworker has been carrying out a series of observations with David to get to know his play preferences. She has noticed that he likes to be outdoors and play with the sieve in the sand pit. However, rather than allowing the sand to fall through the sieve, David likes to twist the sieve deep into the sand. He is excited when he sees the sand coming up through the holes. David also likes wheeled vehicles such as bicycles and prams but he likes to turn them upside down and spin the wheels. On another occasion, David chooses a hoop and takes it on a 'walk' rolling it all over the outdoor yard and over the rope bridge. His keyworker chats with David's mum when she comes to collect him and she recounts David's preference for anything round. Mum tells her that at home David loves to sit and watch the washing machine spinning around and motor racing on the TV. The keyworker recognises that David has a rotational schema and decides to discuss ways of providing activities to nuture David's schema at the next planning meeting. The key worker ensures that there are resources provided both indoors and outdoors to support David's rotational schema. She keeps careful observational notes of David and uses terminology that feds into this schema, such as: round, twirls, rolls and twists. Activities are planned that facilitate David's schema such as throwing numbered bean bags into a hoop and totalling the numbers that land inside. Outdoors David is encouraged to paint water circles on the shed to develop his hand eye coordination and fine motor skills. The key worker is able to develop David's skills across the curriculum by ensuring that he is having fun and learning through his schema. She regularly updates David's mother on his schematic development.

Question to Consider:

1. Think of one of the schemas discussed. Can you use the observation cycle to plan for it?

Conclusion

This chapter has given an overview of the history of schemas. It has charted the journey from Piaget as the originator of schemas, up to the contemporary authors who have taken his work forward. Schemas are now part of early childhood education curricula and practitioners are better informed on how schemas can support a child's thinking and knowledge construction. Observation is key to recognising a child's schema and there are a number of resources available to support settings in planning for children's schemas once recognised. Questions have been posed throughout the chapter to facilitate the link between theory and practice along with a case study. The chapter ends with some reflective questions and opportunities for further reading.

Reflective Questions

1. Having read this chapter, can you think of any children you know that have a particular schema?
2. Can you think of ways you or your setting can support children's schemas, such as providing resources and activities? Use the tookit to help you.
3. How can you share knowledge of children's schemas with their parents or caregivers?

Opportunities for Further Reading

- The Pen Green Schema Group (Edited by Cath Arnold) (2023) Schemas in the Early Years. London, Routledge.

This book is written by several practitioners and researchers and each chapter focuses on a different aspect of schemas. It really considers children at the centre of learning.

- Boulton and Thomas (2022b) Schematic development and the curriculum for funded non-maintained nursery settings: toolkit. Available via: https://hwb.gov.wales/repository/resource/39397e24-d5e9-4b57-ad15-09f64f4ad0ec/en/overview

Look at this toolkit as it offers ways to plan for children's schemas along with ideas for learning opportunities, key vocabulary and resources.

References

Arnold, C., The Pen Green Team. (2010). *Understanding schemas and emotion*. London: SAGE.
Atherton, F., & Nutbrown, C. (2013). *Understanding schemas and young children*. London: SAGE.
Athey, C. (1990). *Extending thought in young children: A parent–teacher partnership*. London: Paul Chapman.
Athey, C. (2007). *Extending thought in young children: A parent–teacher partnership* (2nd ed.). London: SAGE.
Athey, C. (2013). Beginning with the theory about schemas. In C. Arnold (Ed.), *Mairs K and The Pen Green Team young children learning through schemas* (pp. 5–16). London: Routledge.
Boulton, P., & Thomas, A. (2022a). How does play in the outdoors afford opportunities for schema development in young children? *International Journal of Play*. https://doi.org/10.1080/21594937.2022.2069348
Boulton, P., & Thomas, A. (2022b). *Schematic development and the curriculum for funded non-maintained nursery settings: Toolkit*. Available via: https://hwb.gov.wales/repository/resource/39397e24-d5e9-4b57-ad15-09f64f4ad0ec/en/overview. Accessed 31 October 2023.
Bruce, T. (2011). *Early childhood education* (4th ed.). London: Hodder Education.
Constable, K. (2013). *Planning for Schematic Learning in the Early Years*. Oxon: Routledge.
Education Scotland. (2020). *Realising the ambition: Being me*. Education Scotland.
England, L. (2018). *Schemas—A Practical Handbook*. London: Bloomsbury.

Halpenny, A., & Pettersen, J. (2014). *Introducing Piaget*. Oxon: Routledge.
Louis, S. (2016). *The importance of schemas in every child's learning*. Available via: https://www.communityplaythings.co.uk/learning-library/articles/schemas-by-stella-louis. Accessed 29 April 2024.
Louis, S., Beswick, C., Magraw, L., Hayes, L., & Featherstone, S. (2008). *Again! Again! Understanding schemas in young children*. A &C Black Publishers Limited.
Maynard, T., & Thomas, N. (2009). *Early childhood studies* (2nd ed.). London: SAGE.
Meade, A., & Cubey, P. (2008). *Thinking children, learning about schemas*. Berkshire, Open University.
Nutbrown, C. (2006). *Key concepts in early childhood education and care*. London: SAGE.
Nutbrown, C. (2011). *Threads of thinking schemas and young children's learning* (4th ed.). London: SAGE.
Piaget, J. (1953). *The origins of intelligence in the child* (2nd ed.). London: Routledge and Kegan Paul.
Piaget, J. (1959). *The language and thought of the child*. London: Routledge and Kegan Paul.
Piaget, J. (1962). *Play, dreams and imitation in childhood*. London: Routledge and Kegan Paul.
Piaget, J. (1969). *The mechanisms of perception*. London: Routledge and Kegan Paul.
Piaget, J. (1970). *Science of education and the psychology of the child*. Harlow: Longman.
Piaget, J. (1972). *The principles of genetic epistemology*. London: Routledge and Kegan Paul.
Piaget, J. (1973). *The child and reality: Problems of genetic psychology*. New York: Grossman Publishers.
Piaget, J., & Inhelder, B. (1969). *The psychology of the child: Translated from the French by Helen Weaver*. New York: Basic Books.
Prodger, A. (2013). A case study about Jack. In C. Arnold (Ed.), *Mairs K and The Pen Green Team. Young children learning through schemas* (pp. 58–78). Routledge.
Sunderland, P. (1992). *Cognitive development today: Piaget and his critics*. London: Paul Chapman.
The Pen Green Schema Group. (2023). *Schemas in the early years*. Cath Arnold (Ed.). Routledge.
Thomas, A. (2018a). *Planning for schemas in the Welsh curriculum*. Available via: https://hwb.gov.wales/repository/resource/e0ef76fe-334f-45ae-a6c8-7aa630e64310. Accessed 31 October 2023.
Thomas, A. (2018b). *Exploring the role of schemas within the Welsh Foundation Phase curriculum*. Unpublished doctoral dissertation. University of South Wales.
Vygotsky, L. S. (1978). *Mind in society*. London: Harvard.
Welsh Government WG. (2020b). *Curriculum for Wales*. Available via: https://hwb.gov.wales/api/storage/4be12be2-3180-4619-963d-b62c4f252423/Toolkit%20supporting%20schemas.pdf. Accessed Sept 2023.
Welsh Government (WG). (2022a). *A curriculum for funded non-maintained nursery settings*. Available via: https://hwb.gov.wales/curriculum-for-wales/designing-your-curriculum/developing-a-vision-for-curriculum-design/ (Accessed 31 October 2023).
Welsh Government (WG). (2022b). *Schematic development: noticing and supporting the repeated patterns of behaviour in children's play*. Available via: View—Hwb (gov.wales) (Accessed 31 October 2023).
Welsh Government (WG). (2023a). *Observation*. Available via: https://hwb.gov.wales/playlists/view/7bab8694-79a1-4a14-8288-3f8c3b530358/en/1?options=CNIQ39k7rbEp4zsz8OdGxip83XDxyAM%252BxyuNqUgoOrvEtxGXwma9Q0UtNK7LrNnQnL8NVHxkwcu%252BPl0Q%252Bs3r%252BpBj7RHxupfLA7IsLWUM1Bz485n2Qo%252FPbqLi7RFnkpOEnjl6w4I3Gfo7cgg4Yzgwslw%252BWgsRr9dJwMFnueYRanBVabtK7h5psKRfM1P3LDZ5WZfh0s92lJ9WlbxC7KgvbQ%253D%253D (Accessed 01 December 2023).

Chapter 3
Outdoor Pedagogy in Early Childhood Education

Outdoor Learning

Outdoor learning and teaching can be defined in many ways and includes opportunities for outdoor play, environmental education, adventure & recreational activities, and outdoor education and can encompass personal development programmes and more. (English Outdoor Council, 2018). Whilst there are no clear defined boundaries there are common elements to outdoor learning which underpin its importance as a pedagogy, particularly in Early Childhood Education. Outdoor learning:

- Values direct experiences and is an active participatory way to learn.
- Embraces the natural environment, where children learn to care and connect with nature.
- Engages all the senses, making learning real and bringing learning alive.
- Offers varied opportunities to support the national curriculum and broaden horizons.
- Unlocks potential, allowing children to discover, be curious, take risks and develop self-efficacy, developing their understanding of the world and how it works

The Context of Outdoor Pedagogy

The values and importance of outdoor learning and play, particularly in Early Childhood Education (ECE) are and have been demonstrated and researched by pioneers such as Macmillan, Montessori, Steiner and Froebel (Tovey, 2007). The importance of the outdoor environment as a 'classroom' was championed by these pioneers because of its potential to foster children's independence, encouraging active learning, experiential opportunities, contact with nature and the outdoors and opportunities to support all aspects of child development (Constable, 2015).

Outdoor learning/play and outdoor provision are terms used interchangeably within the context of ECE. Definitions of this teaching approach are diverse and varied and can mean different things to different people. The dominant pedagogy most often observed in ECE still includes high levels of structure, teacher-led learning and prescribed whole-class activities indoors; it represents a teaching method rather than a pedagogy informed by values and context. This is predicated on the tensions that arise between 'Excellence over Enjoyment' and 'values versus actions' (Waite, 2010; Bennet et al., 1997).

Outdoor learning can be defined as a planned learning activity that may be organised within the confines of the school environment and beyond, including playful encounters with materials, objects and equipment. However, some practitioners will view outdoor provision as 'playtime' spent outdoors where children 'let off steam' (Bilton & Waters, 2016). Or indeed a separate 'subject' or 'bolt on' that is sometimes offered as a reward. However, outdoor provision can provide a dramatic contrast to the indoor classroom. Through skilled teaching, interpretation and facilitation, outdoor experiences readily become a stimulating source of fascination, personal growth and breakthroughs in learning for many children (IOL, 2025 https://www.outdoor-learning.org/about/about-outdoor-learning.html).

Benefits of Outdoor Learning and Teaching

The use of the outdoor environment as a landscape for learning and play provides many benefits to children's learning and development (WAG, 2009). The Institute for Outdoor Learning (IOL) (2025) suggests there are links between schools offering regular and long-term outdoor learning opportunities and the potential for children to achieve a range of outcomes in health and wellbeing, connections to nature, self-efficacy and confidence as well as cognitive learning. Essentially, outdoor learning is an experiential approach and as such enables children to problem solve and make sense of everyday real-life experiences where they can develop imagination and creativity and allows them to decipher a sense of place within their living world.

The outdoors offers authentic experiences and has the power to help children make meaning of the world, retaining what they learn because of the affordances of the learning environment.

Benefits of learning outdoors are well documented and suggest that the outdoor environment engages children in deep learning and develops physical, cognitive, social and emotional aspects of their development (Bilton & Waters, 2016; Brussoni et al., 2015). Outdoor learning and play allow children to develop physical coordination, balance and control; the physical benefits of children learning and playing outside are plentiful, including developing balance, flexibility and coordination. Gross motor movement improves and subsequently continues to develop bone density, all of which lead to children developing their fine motor skills enabling them to hold a paintbrush or pencil. These aspects of physical development cannot be isolated from the benefits to cognitive development in the early years and cognitive development may not always be as overt as that of physical development but there are significant elements of cognition required to physically, as well as emotionally engage with all that the outdoors affords children. Open and unstructured play allows a child's brain to recharge; free play enables children to think creatively where their actions and ideas are steered by their imaginations (ISM, 2018).

Being and learning in the natural outdoor environment can be made up of small but significant experiences that afford children 'everyday adventures'. It provides unpredictable but essential elements of growing up, of making judgements about their physical abilities, taking risks as well as making friends. But these elements depend on being 'out and about' and not being closeted indoors (Gill, 2007). The outdoor environment can stimulate the senses far more than an indoor learning environment (Carson, 1956) and when learning is active and made real through use of all the senses, the greater the long-term retention of that constructed knowledge (Clarke, 2006), so it is consequently more memorable for the learner.

Learning through the senses is fundamental in early learning, experiences that we have in the early years affect the architecture of the brain, and thus over time a child's brain is built based on their experiences. Building a solid brain architecture is something that children cannot do on their own; they need the support of an enabling adult and an effective environment to provide the nurture they need to influence positive development (Alberta Family Wellness, 2013). The natural outdoor environment which utilises all the senses helps to build the neural pathways and organise information in the brain for later reference. This is part of how children fathom the world around them and is the stem of cognitive development, the mental processes that take place in the brain, including thinking, attention, language, learning, memory and perception. These processes are not isolated abilities—they are a raft of different, interacting skills which together allow us to function in a holistic fashion, eventually as healthy adults. The work of Piaget underpins the need for children (and adults) to adjust their thinking continually, in terms of new ideas and acquired knowledge. He believed that nature and nurture contributed to intellectual ability and stressed that children needed to be active learners (Piaget 1972; Maynard & Thomas, 2009) and as such children organise their knowledge and understanding of the world into cognitive structures called schemas (Piaget 1953, 1959, 1970).

Maynard et al. (2013) identified changes in behaviour of children and staff during outdoor learning and play. Staff were more relaxed in their approach and children were much calmer than they were normally. Therefore, the benefits are tangible for both children and the adults that facilitate learning and play in outdoor spaces. It is maintained that outdoor spaces offer freedom not just to play in more space and on a larger scale but to think in an unhurried way and this can apply to the child as well as the adult. Therefore, children can move more freely, play on a larger scale and experience at first hand the world around them (Beyer et al., 2015; Bilton, 2002; Ouvry, 2003), whilst the adult can observe and view the natural environment as the 'third teacher' allowing it to guide the child, as the slowness enables the learning to percolate to suit the pace of the child. This slowness of learning (Clark 2023) will be explored later in the chapter.

Challenges of Outdoor Provision

A Fear of the Term 'Pedagogy' Used Outdoors?

How we perceive pedagogy is key to our practice and in the outdoors, it is connected to how the practitioner perceives nature. Using nature as part of our pedagogy is to teach alongside nature/environment and the learner (Cree & Robb, 2021). The term pedagogy is important because it raises the value of the actual experience of what occurs when a child is learning in the outdoor environment. The term 'it's only play' is often heard, yet play is a powerful vehicle for learning (Gray, 2013). It also means that pedagogical practices used in nature enable practitioners to develop their knowledge and expertise, from which they can confidently communicate how and what learning looks like outdoors. A lack of knowledge and experience can limit the perspective required to understand what is taking place in front of you as a practitioner; this is referred to as 'Pedagogical blindness' (Cree & Robb, 2021). This is particularly relevant when we consider Schematic development in children. We rely on what we are used to and often base our ideas on assumptions of what we already know, but a deeper understanding of how children make sense of the world and the ways in which they learn is needed along with the need to observe mindfully.

Waite (2020, p. 1) suggests that school-based outdoor learning involves 'play, teaching and learning that takes place in natural environments for children in formal education and care settings'. Classroom based learning is further extended when using local parks, playgrounds which enhances the authenticity of the experiences and creates more memorable learning opportunities for the learner (James & Williams, 2017). It brings physical benefits through active learning and can support teaching across curriculum areas of learning (MacQuarrie, 2018).

> **Case Study:** At MB nursery, practitioners discussed how their improved knowledge of schemas has helped them to better support a child's development. Following some training and support through provision of training materials on how to observe and recognise dynamic schemas in young children, and developing their outdoor environment by providing a range of loose parts where the children had free flow access to these outdoor resources, they better understood what was happening and how to support the child.
>
> In the garden section of the outdoor spaces, one child was always drawn to play with the soil, digging and filling the wheel barrow with soil and moving it from place to place. Initially L said: "at first we thought he was just fixated on the soil, but after observing him for several weeks, we realised that he was fascinated by moving objects from one place to another. Although he moved objects indoors, it didn't appear to allow him the space he needed and we realised that as soon as he was outdoors he was demonstrating a repeated pattern of behaviour once he was given the space and the agency to do what he needed… I think the freedom freed up his thinking …."

L went on to say: "because of our improved understanding it was apparent that he had a transporting schema and his need to move things around but particularly outdoors allowed him to make decisions, move safely and develop his social as well as his communication skills, this was obvious once we made the connection—when he was outside in the soil and mud he was engrossed in what he was doing" (Fig. 3.1).

Fig. 3.1 Child pushing wheelbarrow: Noticing a Transporting Schema

We will revisit this case study later in Chapter 8.

Thus, access to training and developing new knowledge to keep practice fresh and relevant as well as to help think more consciously about what takes place in front of our very eyes can help to remove 'pedagogical blindspots' (Cree & Robb, 2021). Unless practitioners are able to view pedagogy through a different lens and understand what learning and development is taking place when children learn and play in the outdoors, it will always be a challenge to actively include 'outdoor pedagogy' as an essential part of provision.

Viewing Outdoor Learning as a Pedagogy to Teach the Curriculum

The importance of children and young people learning outdoors is considered a valuable vehicle for learning and development and is acknowledged nationally and internationally; however, the 'privilege' varies across the globe (Prince & Diggory, 2023). In many countries, government policy supports 'outdoor learning as a pedagogy' that is integrated within curricula and is a regular part of provision and this means that the *teaching and the learning* takes place in the natural outdoor environment. This is particularly prevalent in Scandinavia, where the Forest School approach is common in the early years in Denmark, along with Udeskole (Mygind et al., 2019) and experiential education in the natural outdoor environment is part of the Finnish national curriculum (Sjoblom & Svens, 2019). In the UK, Scotland includes outdoor learning as a mandatory aspect of the Curriculum for excellence (Learning & Teaching Scotland, 2010).

However, in some nations outdoor learning can often be seen as a 'bolt on' to the formal curriculum, as it is not identified as mandatory in policy, nor is it considered a 'natural' approach to learning and teaching as perhaps Scandinavian cultures do. Outdoor learning is non-mandatory in the English and Welsh Curricula. Subjects such as Physical Education or Health Education sometimes provide the justification for opportunities for outdoor learning (Leather, 2018; Prince & Cory-Wright, 2022), in light of children being active, and often outside, where children learn different sport skills or are involved in 'adventure' education such as orienteering and outdoor recreational activities. These activities, whist beneficial, are generally focused on developing physical skills related to the PE curriculum and do not focus on a more holistic approach to learning where, for example, language, number, science and expressive arts skills might be identified as key outcomes of the outdoor learning experiences. Thus, some educators would see outdoor learning as a much more useful vehicle with considerably wider scope (IOL, 2025). Thus, the general lack of recognising outdoor learning as a holistic pedagogy across the age range is a missed opportunity for children to make connections between real-life experiences that traverse the subjects/areas of learning. This of course also relies on practitioners' own ability and skills to teach children in the outdoors, and where their motivation for using the outdoor environment as an extension of the indoor classroom is underpinned with relevant training and resources that enable them to be confident in their practice. This may be an area that presents barriers to outdoor learning being offered as a consistent, quality teaching and learning experience and needs addressing through initial teacher training and ECE degree programmes.

Therefore, it is important that student teachers, teachers and teacher educators experience the natural environment themselves, in ways that allow them to linger and experience the unexpected in their learning and where a pedagogical development of the whole person 'head, heart and lifestyle' (Aoki 1983 in Clark 2023) becomes critical in shaping the approaches that are used in ECE. This affects a practitioner's own understanding of nature as much as it does the children that they will teach. Opportunities to experience the natural world through slow pedagogy that promotes student teachers' knowledge and skills are an important part of their professional development (Palmberg et al., 2018 cited in Wolf et al., 2022). Thus, in the same way, outdoor pedagogy needs to be embedded by the teacher educator in the delivery of the HE curriculum, in order for the student teacher to become familiar and confident in implementing it in their own practice and understanding that it has an equal place in supporting a holistic curriculum.

In England and Wales, however, outdoor play does have a place within the Early Years curricula, as it is recognised as a fundamental element of children's development and learning. In England the Early Years Foundation Stage (EYFS, birth—5 years) states that access to outdoor learning and play and provision of planned outdoor activities every day is a statutory requirement [Department for Education, (DfE), 2021]. The Curriculum for Wales (CfW) guidance, for 3–16 years; (WG, 2020a) refers to 'outdoor learning/environment' on several occasions, often in conjunction with 'indoor' opportunities within a range of the Areas of Learning and Experience (AoLE), using 'should' as its expectation, but it is not statutory. Having access to outdoor areas does not ensure that children are engaged in meaningful and authentic outdoor/nature experiences and in many cases outdoor learning and play is not afforded to children due to systemic barriers and practitioners feeling challenged (Oberle et al., 2021; Waite, 2020) connected to a neoliberal culture within practice. Therefore, in Wales, ECE practitioners are guided by curricula that encourages them to 'ensure' that outdoor learning is a fundamental approach to children's early learning experiences. The learning environment is a key enabler for the curriculum and should allow all learners of all ages to experience authentic learning opportunities outdoors as well as indoors (WG, 2020a, p. 51). It also notes that in the early stages of progression, learning through extended periods of play and open-ended exploration should 'prioritise outdoor opportunities' (WG, 2020b, p. 51).

In addition, the Curriculum for Funded Non-Maintained Nurseries (NMCfN) for 0–3years in Wales (WG, 2022a) places 'outdoor learning and play' as central to the approach for EY provision and provides useful guidance to practitioners. At preschool level and within the NMCfN, there is a clear connection between the learning environment and pedagogy (WG, 2022a, p. 15) and the links are specific in several places within the curriculum document. Pedagogy is directly linked to 'consistent' opportunities for learning 'being outdoors' and benefits of this are clearly highlighted, supporting physical, social, emotional and spiritual development including wellbeing (WG, 2022a, p. 16). This appears to be the first time that 'outdoor learning and play' have been overtly associated with 'pedagogy' in Welsh national curricula.

Furthermore, the NMCfN also includes a clear overview of Schemas and their important role in early learning. Here schemas are defined as 'a child repeating an activity over and over again, for example, tipping over containers or making circles in the sand …. These repetitive actions support vital brain development and are called schemas (WG, 2022a, p. 38)'. The inclusion of this clear overview illustrates significant progress in educational policy in Wales, not only in recognising the importance of Schematic development in child development but also in ensuring that EY practitioners are aware of and understand what schemas are, their prominence in helping children to make sense of the world around them and the importance and value of observations in supporting practitioners to identify and thus plan opportunities to support children's schematic development (see Chapter 2 on observing schemas for further support with this).

Natural Environments Versus The Clock and the Timetable

The effectiveness of schools in England and Wales is measured by government inspectorate, Ofsted and Estyn, respectively. Details of how schools are measured are far too great to discuss here but ultimately based on a range of criteria schools are ranked as a consequence of their inspection, which inevitably leads to a highly pressurised workforce. Evidence suggests that inspection drives provision and can influence the quality of outdoor provision (Prince & Diggory, 2023). To receive a grading of 'good' children, should have the opportunity to go outside and take part in physical activity, as well as experience risk and challenge outdoors (Ofsted 2022). However, this mostly appears in PE to improve health and wellbeing as outdoor learning (OL) is not mandatory and not recognised as a 'pedagogy' to teach the whole curriculum. For OL to be implemented as a pedagogy that supports the delivery of the curriculum, headteachers need to be sure that the provision of OL will be viewed as a pedagogy that contributes positively to the 'good outcome' of an Ofsted grading (Prince & Diggory, 2023). Hence its value necessitates recognition and the profession, and the inspectorate has to believe in it as a purposeful learning and teaching approach across all areas of learning.

As an adjunct to this, OL is likely to be supplanted by the pressures of the standards set, of 'performativity' particularly in regard to subject outcomes such as literacy and numeracy. The downward pressure to meet curriculum outcomes competes against 'slower pedagogies' to ensure that children are meeting the required outcomes within the expected timeframe; this is a significant pressure on teaching time. Thus, as outdoor learning embraces learning through discovery, curiosity and exploration all of which require time for knowledge to be constructed and assimilated, it loses its place in teaching and learning, if it ever had a place, and 'time' becomes the barrier to outdoor pedagogy providing a rich, deep, holistic learning experience for children to 'wallow' in their play and make sense of it (Bruce, 2012).

This approach aligns with Alison Clark's work (2023) on Slow knowledge and its importance in allowing children to follow their interests, to develop curiosity as they learn at their pace and make sense of the world around them. Outdoor learning is a slow pedagogy, and schematic development also develops slowly and deeply. These experiences value unexpected turns and take different directions, embracing time to explore, question and not be driven by targets. Both require deep observation from the adult and so they neither should be hurried by time, as 'Hurried teachers can result in hurried children' (Carlsen & Clark 2022). Clark's (2023) research powerfully presents the arguments for the need to consider how educators need to 'stretch time', and indeed question how this can be learned, possibly through training, professional development but perhaps most compellingly through 'professional confidence' (Carlsen & Clark 2022); which is needed to enable educators to 'catch the moment' so we nurture the 'unhurried child' (Clark 2023).

The outdoors lends itself to slow practices and being outside somehow expands time where educators' relationship with time changes, perhaps linked to a release from the pressures of performativity and more about being in the moment with the children and having a sense of place (Clark 2023). It also appears to give permission to educators to relate differently to the children, being less of the leader and more the observer. "Access to natural environments over time can in some ways break the hold of the clock and the timetable" (Clark 2023, p. 64). This is a fundamental approach when considering the opportunities that are provided by the adult to afford children the opportunities for their schemas to be nurtured and for learning to 'percolate' at a pace that is conducive to the individual child.

Research Spotlight

Consider the article cited here:

Carlsen, K. & Clark, A. (2022). Potentialities of pedagogical documentation as an intertwined research process with children and teachers in slow pedagogies, *European Early Childhood Education Research Journal* 30 (2) pp. 200–212, https://doi.org/10.1080/1350293X.2022.2046838

Summary: This is a most useful article for ECE which looks at two small-scale ECE studies in Norway and explores the value of 'pedagogical documentation' and its relationship to slow pedagogy and practices.

Pedagogical documentation in this article refers to the Reggio Emilia philosophy, where it is used as a tool for co-constructing learning journeys, an active participatory tool used between teachers, children and parents. The concept embraces three moments in the continuous 'doings' of everyday ECE: observation, documentation and interpretation. This process as explained in the article offers an insight into children's actions and their development, but more importantly it connects to how this concept can be seen as a slow pedagogical practice where time is suspended, and learning is transformative. It highlights some of the tensions in and around curricula frameworks and policy and the discrepancies between testing and explorative, slower learning processes. Further illuminating discussions from the small studies offered highlight the contention of 'Hurried children' and the relationship between 'catching the moment' and 'stretched time' in practice, giving children and practitioners a 'chance to breathe'. It does however require professional skill and confidence, which can be challenging and has implications for EC teacher education, so students can experience stretched time within the demands of teaching for outcomes. It makes us think about whose rhythm and pace we are prioritising.

After you have read the article, consider the following questions in relation to your own experiences and practices:

1. What does your role look like in relation to the pedagogical documentation described in this article?
2. What does slow pedagogy look like for you and your practice?

(a) Are children given time to go off track?
(b) Explore their own interests? Engage in unexpected directions?
(c) Does it perhaps include regular connection with their outdoor environment?
3. Are you aware of 'catching the moment' and 'stretching time' in your practice? What does it look like?
4. What can you take from this research that might influence your thinking and your practice?

Nature Pedagogy and Nature Connectedness

This brings us to a confluence where methods and spaces for teaching and learning i.e. 'pedagogy' and 'nature' come together and align offering central components of ECE practices known as 'nature pedagogy', and which requires the learners and the practitioners to be connected to their natural environment. Where this happens, nature is valued as a primary factor in the learning process, and teaching and development have nature at the very heart of the experiences offered to the children. This ignites curiosity and exploration of the natural environment and develops an understanding of and connection to the natural world. Nature pedagogy is the practice of teaching alongside nature and the learner where children are noticed and their voices are heard, their interests are valued and where the adult although aware, at times is invisible but at other times offers support, providing a safe space and an authentic relationship with the child as well as with the environment (Cree & Robb, 2021). The relationship is with 'place' as much as it is with people.

The research of Wilson (1984) and Gardener (1999) helps us to understand the value of play in natural environments. Wilson's work on Biophilia (1984) suggests that humans have an affinity with natural environment, and he described it as the 'urge to affiliate with other forms of life'. Biophilia is a biological mechanism which is necessary for human development and suggests that learning and play in natural environments align with the innate need of children, nurturing holistic development. Gardner's (1999) multiple intelligence theory further explains 'naturalistic intelligence' or 'nature smart' as interpreted by Louv (2009, p. 203), which supports this connection to the outdoor environment in children's learning and which provides a rich environment for healthy growth and development (Pickering, 2017).

In the same way, 'Nature connectedness' is an appreciation and value for all life that transcends any objective use of nature for humanity's purposes (Zelenski & Nisbet, 2012). It is different for every individual being a subjective construct, based on social and personal influences, but comprised of cognitive (Mayer & Franz, 2004), affective (Schultz, 2001), learnt, experiential and personality (Hinds & Sparks, 2008) factors that when combined, can create a connection with nature. Connecting with nature is also cultivated by knowing and understanding the living things that surround us and knowing the names of different plants and animals can cultivate a connection with that species, spiking an interest in its habitat and thus the lifecycles of nature. Opportunities to connect with nature need time, uninterrupted opportunities to explore and for slow knowledge to percolate the temporal dimensions.

White (2023a) refers to 'Ecological identity' as a phrase that embodies 'nature connectedness' but goes further than just being connected. Ecological identity is about 'being with' nature and not just 'in nature'. In a similar vein to Froebel and Clark, it suggests that children need to be provided with the time and opportunity to linger or wallow (Bruce, 2012) in their outdoor play, almost as though nature becomes the play partner.

To further explore the concepts of how Froebel's philosophy embraces the slow pedagogical approach that values relationships between the child, the adult and environment see the very useful document accessible via the Froebel Trust website (Green & Clark, 2024).[1]

Just as a child develops a relationship with their teacher/adult as a play partner, so they do the same with natural spaces, which given time enables the relationship to be one that is reciprocal 'we look after nature and nature looks after us' (White, 2023a). She likens the feeling of intensity with the natural world as a critical element for children to learn to look after the planet and perhaps explains why children are so compelled to 'dig' because of the connection that is made with the soil and the earth and perhaps feeling part of nature itself. Thus, ecological identity is a bond with nature where it can be seen as the 'responder to the child's play need'.

Therefore, the role of the adult in teaching children plays a significant part in helping children to retain that connection to their natural environment and to further develop an appreciation for nature. The adult must, therefore, also understand the opportunities that are available through the natural environment to support a child's learning and development. Where an adult has experienced nature personally, they are more likely to embrace the outdoors as part of their teaching provision, so that they can facilitate the opportunities that nature offers to the child. This draws upon the work of Rachel Carson's text 'A sense of Wonder' (1956). Her work awakens the 'ancient longing for unity with the living world' (p. 9). Children need to experience the awe and wonder of nature, and she reminds us that we are all part of nature.

> If a child is to keep alive his inborn sense of wonder.... He needs the companionship of at least one adult who can share it, rediscovering with him the joy, excitement, and mystery of the world we live in. (p. 55)

Conclusion

The concepts of outdoor learning and play are fundamental to the holistic development of children, and they are underpinned by several theories and philosophies that advocate for the place of children learning in nature so that they might feel connected and part of the natural environment in which they are growing up.

Curriculum guidelines attempt to highlight the importance of the outdoor environment and its place in the learning experiences of the child. However, tensions

---

[1] https://www.froebel.org.uk/uploads/documents/FT_Slow-Pedagogy_pamphlet.pdf.

exist between academic excellence versus enjoyment in learning and require learner and practitioner to build a relationship with the natural environment in order to value a 'nature pedagogy' approach that holds its own in teaching children effectively and where children learn holistically.

The curriculum does imply however that to fulfil the 'should's' practitioners will need to be open to new ways of learning themselves, considering the outdoors as another pedagogical approach to teaching the curriculum, enabling authentic, experiential and engaging learning experiences for children. It must be a place where schematic development is afforded because of the practitioner's knowledge and understanding of time and space in how children learn and develop, but this is likely to require additional support and training. This approach is also about investing in the future generations to foster a connection to nature and the outdoor environment and to avoid it being displaced by the pressures of a twenty-first-century curriculum. Chapter four will look at what an outdoor enabling environment offers to support Schematic development and considers the theories that underpin this provision, which can give practitioners confidence in employing an outdoor pedagogy in their early childhood practices.

References

Alberta Family Wellness. (2013). *How brains are built: The core story of brain development*. Available on: Youtube Bing Videos. (Accessed: November 2023).

Bennett, N., Wood, E., & Rogers, S. (1997). *Teaching through play: Teachers' thinking and classroom practice*. Open University Press.

Beyer, K., Bizub, J., Szabo, A., Heller, B., Kistner, A., Shawgo, E., & Zetts, C. (2015). Development and validation of the attitudes toward outdoor play scales for children. *Journal of Social Sciences and Medicine, 133*, 253–260.

Bilton, H. (2002). *Outdoor play in the early years: Management and innovation* (2nd ed.). London: David Fulton Publishers.

Bilton, H., & Waters, J. (2016). Why take young children outside? A critical consideration of the professed aims for outdoor learning in the early years by teachers from England and Wales. *Journal of Social Sciences*. https://doi.org/10.3390/socsci6010001

Bruce, T. (2012). *Early childhood practice: A guide for professionals and carers*. Sage.

Brussoni, M., Gibbons, R., Gray, C., Ishikawa, T., Sandseter, E., Bienenstock, A., Chabot, G., Fuselli, P., Herrington, S., Janssen, I., Pickett, W., Power, M., Stanger, N., Sampson, M., & Tremblay, M. S. (2015). What is the relationship between risky outdoor play and health in children? A systematic review. *International Journal of Environmental Research and Public Health, 12*, 6423–6454.

Carlsen, K., & Clark, A. (2022). Potentialities of pedagogical documentation as an intertwined research process with children and teachers in slow pedagogies. *European Early Childhood Education Research Journal, 30*(2), 200–212. https://doi.org/10.1080/1350293X.2022.2046838

Carson, R. (1956). *The sense of wonder*. Harper Collins.

Clark, A. (2023). *Slow knowledge and the unhurried child*. Routledge.

Clarke, S. (2006). *Mills and millipedes*. Benefits of using urban settings for outdoor learning activities. Synergy Learning. Available via: http://www.synergylearning.org. Accessed July 2023.

References

Constable, K. (2015). *The outdoor classroom in practice, ages 3–7: A month-by-month guide to forest school provision*. Routledge.

Cree, J., & Robb, M. (2021). *The essential guide to forest school and nature pedagogy*. Routledge.

English Outdoor Council. (2018). *What is outdoor learning?* Available via: English Outdoor Council: What is Outdoor Learning? Accessed September 2023.

Gardner, H. (1999). *Intelligence reframed: Multiple intelligences for the 21st century*. Basic Books.

Gill, T. (2007). *No fear: Growing up in a risk averse society*. Calouste Gulbenkian Foundation.

Gray, P. (2013). *Free to learn*. Basic Books.

Green, D., & Clark, A. (2024). *A Froebelian approach time for Chidlhood: A slow pedagogy*. Available via: https://www.froebel.org.uk/uploads/documents/FT_Slow-Pedagogy_pamphlet.pdf. Accessed January 2025.

Hinds, J., & Sparks, P. (2008). Engaging with the natural environment: The role of affective connection and identity. *Journal of Environmental Psychology., 28*, 109–120.

Institute of Outdoor Learning. (2025). *What is outdoor learning?* Available via: https://www.outdoor-learning.org/about/about-outdoor-learning.html. Accessed September 2023.

International School of Macao (ISM). (2018). *Outdoor Play and Child Development*. Available via: https://tis.edu.mo/news/outdoor-play-and-child-development. Accessed October, 2022.

James, J. K., & Williams, T. (2017). School-based experiential outdoor education: A neglected necessity. *The Journal of Experiential Education, 40*(1), 58–71. https://doi.org/10.1177/1053825916676190

Learning and Teaching Scotland. (2010). *Curriculum for excellence through outdoor learning*. Available via: https://education.gov.scot/documents/cfe-through-outdoor-learning.pdf. Accessed December 2023.

Leather, M. (2018). Outdoor education in the national curriculum: The shifting sands in formal education. In P. B. Becker, C. L. Humberstone, & J. Schirp (Eds.), *The changing world of outdoor learning in Europe* (pp. 179–193). London: Routledge.

Louv, R. (2009). *Last child in the woods: Saving our children from nature deficit-disorder*. Atlantic Books.

MacQuarrie, S. (2018). Everyday teaching and outdoor learning: Developing an integrated approach to support school-based provision. *Education 3–13, 46*(3), 45–361. https://doi.org/10.1080/03004279.2016.1263968

Mayer, F. S., & Frantz, C. M. (2004). The connectedness to nature scale: A measure of individuals' feeling in community with nature. *Journal of Environmental Psychology., 24*, 503–515.

Maynard, T., & Thomas, N. (2009). *Early childhood studies* (2nd ed.). Sage.

Maynard, T., Waters, J., & Clement, J. (2013). Child-initiated learning, the outdoor environment and the 'underachieving' child. *Early Years: An International Research Journal, 33*(3), 212–225. https://doi.org/10.1080/09575146.2013.771152

Mygind, E., Bølling, M., & Barfod, K. S. (2019). Primary teachers' experiences with weekly education outside the classroom during a year. *Education 3–13, 47*(5), 599–611. https://doi.org/10.1080/03004279.2018.1513544

Oberle, E., Zeni, M., Munday, F., & Brussoni, M. (2021). Support factors and barriers for outdoor learning in Elementary schools: A systemic perspective. *American Journal of Health Education, 52*(5), 251–265. https://doi.org/10.1080/19325037.2021.1955232

Ofsted. (2022). *Early years inspection handbook*. Available via: https://www.gov.uk/government/publications/early-years-inspection-handbook-pdf. Accessed: December 2023.

Ouvry, M. (2003). *Exercising muscles and minds*. New York: National Children's Bureau.

Piaget, J. (1953). *The origins of intelligence in the child* (2nd ed.). Routledge and Kegan Paul.

Piaget, J. (1959). *The language and thought of the child*. Routledge and Kegan Paul.

Piaget, J. (1970). *Science of education and the psychology of the child*. Longman.

Piaget, J. (1972). *The principles of genetic epistemology*. Routledge and Kegan Paul.

Pickering, S. (2017). *Teaching outdoors creatively*. Routledge.

Prince, H., & Cory-Wright, J. (2022). Outdoor education as a deep education for global sustainability and social justice. In K. Petry & J. de Jong (Eds.), *Education in sport and physical activity: Global perspectives and future directions* (pp. 49–59). Routledge.

Prince, H. E., & Diggory, O. (2023). Recognition and reporting of outdoor learning in primary schools in England. *Journal of Adventure Education and Outdoor Learning*. https://doi.org/10.1080/14729679.2023.2166544

Schultz, P. W. (2001). The structure of environmental concern: Concern for self, other people, and the biosphere. *Journal of Environmental Psychology, 21*, 327–339.

Sjöblom, P., & Svens, M. (2019). Learning in the Finnish outdoor classroom: Pupils' views. *Journal of Adventure Education and Outdoor Learning, 19*(4), 301–314. https://doi.org/10.1080/14729679.2018.1531042

Tovey, H. (2007). *Playing outdoors: Spaces and places, risk and challenge: Spaces and places, risks and challenge*. London: McGraw-Hill Education.

WAG. (2009). *Foundation phase outdoor learning handbook*. Cardiff, Crown copyright.

Waite, S. (2010). Losing our way? The downward path for outdoor learning for children aged 2–11 years. *Journal of Adventure Education and Outdoor Learning, 10*(2), 111–126. https://doi.org/10.1080/14729679.2010.531087

Waite, S. (2020). Where are we going? International views on purposes, practices and barriers in school-based outdoor learning. *Education Sciences, 10*(11), 311. https://doi.org/10.3390/educsci10110311

Welsh Government (WG). (2020a). *Curriculum for Wales Guidance*. Cardiff: Crown copyright.

Welsh Government (WG). (2020b). *Curriculum for Wales*. Available via: https://hwb.gov.wales/curriculum-for-wales/designing-your-curriculum/developing-a-vision-for-curriculum-design . Accessed September 2023.

Welsh Government (WG). (2022a). *A Curriculum for funded non-maintained nursery settings*. Available via: https://hwb.gov.wales/api/storage/b1801d78-38c3-4320-9818-d9996c21aef8/220914-a-curriculum-for-funded-non-maintained-nursery-settings.pdf. Accessed 31 october 2023.

White, J. (2023a). *Ecological identity and childhood outdoor play*. The Outdoor Teacher podcasts [Podcast]. September 25th 2023. Available via: The Wild Minds Podcast | Professor Jan White (theoutdoorteacher.com). Accessed: 26th September 2023.

Wilson, E. O. (1984). *Biophilia: The human bond with other species*. Harvard University Press.

Wolf, C., Kunz, P., & Robin, N. (2022). Emerging themes of research into outdoor teaching in initial formal teacher training from early childhood to secondary education—A literature review. *The Journal of Environmental Education, 53*(4), 199–220. https://doi.org/10.1080/00958964.2022.2090889

Zelenski, J. M., & Nisbet, E. K. (2012). Happiness and feeling connected: The distinct role of nature relatedness. *Environment and Behaviour, 6*(1). Available via: https://doi.org/10.1177/0013916512451901. Accessed: November 2023.

Chapter 4
The Ingredients of Effective Outdoor Environments and How They Can Nurture Schematic Development in Early Childhood

Definition: Effective environments whether indoors or outdoors need to provide authentic experiences for children to learn and develop. Early childhood development is driven by key opportunities to explore and be curious and this enables children to foster an appreciation for the world around them. Opportunities to experience awe and wonder can motivate children's creativity and critical thinking, and communication-rich environments develop language skills further. Thus, a well-planned and considered environment with a broad range of authentic resources will help to facilitate holistic development, including fine and gross motor skills, opportunities for risk and challenge as well as spaces for quieter times. This variety of resources and spaces enables children to embed skills and develop confidence, resilience and self-regulation.

The quality of the play environment has been found to be influential in the enjoyment and benefits that children get from playtime, as well as the different types of play in which they engage (White, 2013). Exploration is a key driver for development in early childhood and it is through exploration that children begin to make sense of the world around them and develop a sense of belonging or 'cynefin' as it is known within the Welsh curricula (WG, 2020a). Children need to engage all of the senses in their learning, and this means that they are more likely to experience awe and wonder which sparks their curiosity about the world; this is the beginning of cognitive development, problem solving and critical thinking upon which schematic development is predicated.

Effective environments encourage communication, develop practical problem solving and nurture mathematical skills in authentic contexts where children can make sense of what is going on around them. Physical development is also supported, and children should be challenged through accessing a wide range of loose parts and open-ended resources which can offer risk and develop resilience, and which enables children to engage with their environment and others, emotionally and socially. Quiet secret spaces are also key to children learning to reflect and contemplate their experiences, where they are not being 'watched' by the teacher (Moore, 2015) and these spaces are particularly powerful outdoors, where we often see children covering themselves over, hiding in small spaces or making dens. Where these behaviours are observed as repetitive, they could be indicators of schematic development.

Qualitative research has demonstrated that the features valued by children in their play environment may not match the assumptions of adults (Gibson Cornell & Gill, 2017). Thus, in order for authentic experiences to be afforded to children, it is essential that we place the child at the centre of the planning and review the effectiveness of the environment and the resources available as a continuous process, so that it becomes an effective environment which nurtures children's development and their wellbeing. This leads us to look at two important concepts that are critical ingredients to effective environments for children's learning and play, that of 'Loose parts play' and 'Affordance Theory'.

Definition Loose parts play (LPP) interventions introduce moveable materials and equipment to children's play spaces to facilitate unstructured, child-led play (Gibson, Cornell & Gill, 2017). Resources and materials deemed **as 'loose parts'** are those that facilitate open-ended play. Nicholson (1972) described them as 'variables' and included things like materials, smells, gases, fluids and music, animals and plants all of which he declared children loved to play with and experiment, becoming 'inventors'.

Resources and materials deemed as 'loose parts' are those that facilitate open-ended play, so like materials that allow affordance, sand, water, large play equipment, diverse types of containers and blocks can be regarded as loose part materials, and they are generally common in an early years outdoor learning environment. The introduction of loose parts into children's play affords significant opportunities for holistic development including physical, social, communication and cognitive development. The theory of 'loose parts' was proposed by architect, Simon Nicholson (1972). Nicholson proposed that loose parts were 'all the things that satisfy one's curiosity and give us the pleasure that results from discovery and invention (1972, p. 30). Nicholson further argued, that in any environment the amount of discovery or creativity a child gets is causally linked to the varied materials made available within it. Thus, the role of the practitioner is critical in observing the needs and the interests of the child in order that the materials and resources made available stimulate and support development, optimising opportunities for children's creativity and engagement, allowing them to make sense of the world.

Loose parts are about real-world learning for all children and young people, and where objects are outdoors, they are generally either larger, messier, require more space to manoeuvre or are simply found naturally in the outdoor environment. The process both of introducing them and of playing with them involves collaboration, sharing, thinking, problem-solving and decision-making where the outcome is

4 The Ingredients of Effective Outdoor Environments and How They Can … 41

evident, … better play experiences (Play Wales, 2017). Loose parts like this allow children to develop body awareness and perception of shape, depth and size as well as orientation (Figs. 4.1 and 4.2).

Example In Fig. 4.1 the children discuss the need to move the wooden wheeled box in certain directions in order to get to another place in the yard. They become more aware of the size of the box and the weight, where each member needs to position themselves in order to move it in the right direction and place their body positions in order to push or pull. The child sitting gives instructions and orientates herself and the group as they move around the space working together (Fig. 4.1).

Fig. 4.1 Moving a Loose part: Manoeuvring a wooden wheeled box across the yard

Example Children need environments they can manipulate and where they can invent, construct, evaluate and modify their own constructions and ideas through play (Fig. 4.2).. Thus, the use of loose parts is a crucial element of children's play in the outdoors and objects such as drainpipes, tyres, wheels, buckets, sticks, and pallets are all stimuli for creative ideas. These can be used for making patterns, transporting objects (transporting schemas in Fig. 4.3), where a cart is being pulled across the yard, and they can indicate how a child's brain interprets the world.

But the theory of loose parts is about more than the materials and the objects; it is a theory about democracy and self-governance, individuals and groups collaborating to shape their world according to their own vision (Hobson, 2020). Thus, when left to their own devices, children will play with whatever is around; it does not need to be costly and usually comes from the recycling bin or someone's garage. Loose parts often reflect the context of the local community and its culture; in an urban community pipes and bricks may be seen, in coastal communities fishing nets might be recycled, in rural places, bales of hay, tyres and tree branches from local fields are often found. Planning is often needed to gather resources and recycled materials so that worn items can be replaced, and objects remain interesting (Play

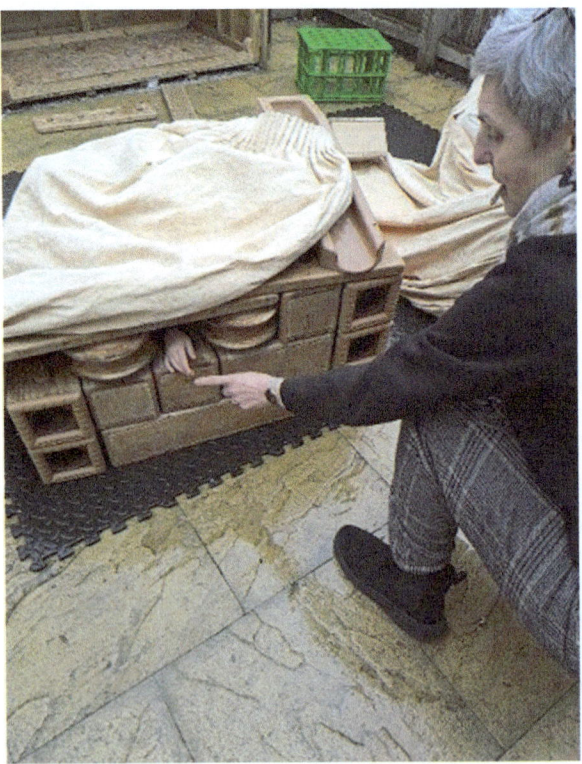

Fig. 4.2 I am hiding in my castle - An Enclosing Schema

Fig. 4.3 A Child pulls a wooden cart containing water jugs across the yard: A Transporting Schema

Wales, 2017). This does require time; however, practitioners need not have anxiety about objects being damaged or lost; this learning in effective outdoor environments is not essentially about the loose parts; it is about how it *affords* richer, deeper play experiences (Hobson, 2020), which helps children to make sense of the world around them, as they demonstrate repeated patterns of behaviour through their play, thus supporting their schematic development (Boulton & Thomas, 2022a).

Research on the Benefits of Loose Parts Play (LPP)

Most studies around the use of loose parts in children's play have focused largely on physical activity outcomes and evidence suggests that loose parts can significantly increase moderate to vigorous activity whilst also decreasing sedentary behaviour (Englen et al., 2013). In addition, evidence regarding how children engage with fixed play resources is mixed, some of which indicates that physical activity decreases, and other research suggests that physical activity increases (Dyment & O'Connell, 2013; Frost, 1990). However, other qualitative studies looking at loose parts play have considered other developmental domains such as social behaviour and cognition

(Lester Jones & Russell, 2010; Maynard and Waters, 2007) and self-esteem and confidence (James, 2012). Based on interviews in schools that implemented loose parts as part of an intervention, Lester et al. (2010) reported benefits to social behaviour and academic performance. In addition, Maynard and Waters (2007) studied child–teacher interactions in outdoor spaces and although the focus of the study was not LPP, they found that approximately a third of the child initiated communications were about the naturally occurring loose parts that they had discovered in their outdoor spaces, which suggests that loose parts do influence social behaviour.

James (2012) also evaluated the impact of loose parts play and posited improvements in self-esteem, confidence, social inclusion and happiness in addition to findings that suggested the children were less bored and less aggressive during playtime. It would seem that as loose parts can offer opportunities for children to share resources and collaborate, then there could be improved outcomes for emotional regulation as well. There is also a connection between Loose parts and risk taking in play (Gill, 2007; Lavyrsen et al. 2017) which improves children's ability to manage risk more effectively, and the work of Bundy et al. (2009) suggests that loose parts can foster social skills and collaboration with peers as collective decisions to manage risk are made collectively. The use of loose parts in the outdoors and risk will be explored in more detail later.

However, the use of loose parts undoubtedly requires physical action in most cases and as several studies indicated earlier, loose parts play is connected to increases in physical activity. Thus, links between physical activity and mental wellbeing (Ahn & Fedewa, 2011) and academic achievement (Singh, 2012) may therefore be indirectly linked to loose parts play where children's increased physical activity is a variable that improves engagement in play and social, emotional and cognitive outcomes.

Recipe: Task—Audit of Your Resources and Loose Parts Pause here and think about the selection of materials and resources that you have available at your setting—identify the loose parts that are found outside and those that are inside which might indicate children's interests and how they are being used by children who are demonstrating repetitive behaviours. E.g. always lining things up, connecting things together or taking things apart, throwing objects or letting things fall from a height or always wanting to make circles, spinning or rotational movement.

It may therefore be useful to complete an audit (see Table 4.1 as an example) and using the headings provided, consider the Loose Parts and other resources you also have that may be fixed, and remember to include the topography (i.e. the 'features of the land'). This can help you:

- consolidate what opportunities are afforded to the children
- how easy it is for the children to access them
- where/how they are meeting the needs and interests of the children
- what changes you may need to make

Table 4.1 An Audit of your Loose Parts and Resources

Fixed equipment	Loose parts	Topography features	How have you seen children use them	Links to schemes
e.g. Climbing bars	e.g. Tyres		Hang upside down	Orientation
			Swing	
			Roll them	Rotational
			Put things inside and drag them	Transporting
			Line them up	Positioning
			Use them as places to keep things	Enclosing
		e.g. hilly/sloping area	Stand on the top and look at different views	Trajectory
			Roll things down them	Orientation
			Roll themselves down them	

This is a very useful Loose Parts Play Toolkit[1] (Casey & Robertson, 2019). It can help you develop your approach in planning and preparing as well as using loose parts to support children's holistic development and therein their schemas too. It offers some very helpful examples and case studies that serve to encourage confidence and understanding of the affordance of loose parts and our role as the adult in those very important play opportunities.

Affordance Theory

Definition American psychologist Gibson (1979) suggested that environments and objects within them have values and meanings that are unique to the person perceiving them. The '**affordances**' of an object or space are all the things it has the 'potential to do or be'.

When children play in a space or with an object, they experience it in a unique way. Rather than its intended purpose, they may view it in terms of its 'affordances'. How children perceive objects may not match adult assumptions and every child will see a value or possibility in a resource or space or object that others may not see. This unique view can help to underpin thinking and patterns of behaviour that can help to nurture children's schemas. Forman (1994) states that different media have different affordances or capacities for representing a concept, and some media provide a greater

---

[1] https://www.playscotland.org/resources/print/Loose-Parts-Play-Tookit-Revised.pdf?plsctml_id=10924.

affordance to be transformed and contends that, 'children learn more deeply when they represent the same concept in different media' (Forman, 1994, p. 41). This can be considered in terms of children's schemas where they choose varied materials to represent their schema or threads of thought (Nutbrown 2011), therefore, the repeated pattern of behaviour is seen manifesting through different materials over time.

How Affordance Theory Underpins Practice

Through different media, children can test out ideas and also design ideas (Forman, 1994). Materials found in the outdoors such as sand, water and large play equipment can afford children lots of diverse ways to use their schemas to construct their knowledge and understanding. Atherton and Nutbrown (2013, p. 42) argue that when Athey talked of 'content and match', where content was chosen to match a child's schema, this can be considered 'Forman's media and affordance'. The affordances provided by being in the outdoors are often 'hidden affordances'. Gaver (1991) expanded Gibson's theory and identified that 'hidden affordances' offer the potential for actions to be taken but are not necessarily perceived by individuals within their environment. One might look at a drainpipe and think, 'that can be used for collecting water'; or it could also be used to transport a ball into another object such as a bucket. Thus, having the freedom and space of being outdoors to manipulate objects and use varied materials that engage the senses in a multi-faceted way affords opportunities for children to develop their schemas. They can construct meaning, knowledge and understanding of the world, in ways that are personal and unique to them. Thus, affordances will vary according to the characteristics of the individuals who interact with the environment.

Understanding affordance theory as an early childhood educator is fundamental to supporting planning and provision. As already mentioned earlier when discussing loose parts, observation plays a key role in identifying the needs and the interests of the child in order that the materials and resources made available stimulate and support development. This optimises opportunities for children's creativity and engagement, allowing them to make sense of the world. Therefore, if practitioners understand the concept of affordance it:

- Guides them in considering the types and variety of materials and loose parts that are provided for the children
- It helps them to consolidate WHY a range of materials need to be provided:
  - Looking at holistic development-cognitive, social, physical and emotional
  - Encouraging different types of play
  - Makes for effective environments for play and learning
- It offers a planning route to meet the individual needs and interests of children

Affordance theory helps educators to see the world through the eyes of the child and it can help to foster agency and to understand that every child will see a unique value in objects that others do not see. This can underpin patterns of behaviour that can help to explore schemas in children's development.

Finally, the work of Taguchi (2011) potentially takes these theories to another level, where I believe the fundamental concepts of loose parts and Affordance are considered together through a relational materialist lens and where material artefacts [Loose parts] encourage creativity and participation, becoming critical elements of the learning environment. Her work examines the everyday engagement of a child playing with sand, and we are challenged to move beyond our 'taken-for-granted' gaze, of a child [active] playing with sand [passive], as it falls from the child's hand. Instead, what we tend *not to see* is the 'damp, grainy sand, evoking a desire to slowly let it run, out of the loosening grip with increasing speed before it falls into the red bucket (Taguchi 2011, p. 37)'. And so, the question arises 'is the girl playing with the sand or the sand playing with the girl?'. Taguchi (2011) suggests that the sand is playing with the girl as much as the girl plays with the sand, and that play occurs *'in-between'* the girl and the sand (p. 38). This work percolates the deep layers of cognitive development that underpins that which we see when we observe schematic development, where a repeated pattern of play may occur when a child, for example, might whisk water in circles with his finger, denoting a rotational schema and as such, an 'assemblage of forces and flows' emerge in the play *'in-between'* the child and the water. The sensory experiences of such an activity may contribute to the immersive engagement between the child and the water, where deep learning can take place, but how the water speaks to the child may also be a critical factor in meaning making and as such transformative learning occurs between them. Thus, the affordance of the water is unique to that child and 'threads of thinking' (Nutbrown 2011) are generated, nurturing schemas.

Effective Outdoor Environments and Schemas

When using Outdoor spaces that include loose parts and where a clear understanding of affordance theory is applied in practice, this can facilitate learning and play and the development of dynamic schemas as well learning related to 'real life experiences' (Boulton & Thomas, 2022a).

Affordance Theory + Loose parts = learning and play that nurtures schematic development in young children

> **Case Study:** Here (Figs. 4.4 and 4.5) we see Milo in the outdoor spaces at his nursery. Observations have identified that Milo loves to dig and relishes the opportunity to dig soil, sometimes sand. He likes to fill containers, empty them and fill them again (Fig. 4.4), sometimes tipping the containers other times emptying the soil using a scoop or trowel. He also likes to scoop water from one container to another. In Fig. 4.5 he bangs on the upside-down jug to make sure all the contents are 'out'. These actions

are repetitive and as such practitioners have ensured that Milo has easy access to a range of containers, jugs and pots. He is also able to dig soil with a scoop or using his hands and he can also get to the water bowl by himself.

Fig. 4.4 Milo filling and emptying containers with soil: A Transporting schema

Effective Outdoor Environments and Schemas

Fig. 4.5 Milo making sure all the soil it out!

Milo uses a range of loose parts to move natural materials, mix them and transport them from one place to another. He is observed filling and emptying most of the time and pausing to look and feel the materials, perhaps taking time to process what is happening. It could be suggested that play is occurring *'in-between'* Milo and the soil, he forms an assemblage with the soil and the container and 'becomes-with' the soil and the container, and the soil 'becomes-with' Milo (Taguchi 2011). There is no hierarchy in the play, as agency and intentionality are distributed between all the 'players', or 'performative agents' (Bennett, 2010). Adults allow Milo the time and space to play in this way, enabling the thinking to be slow and at his pace. An 'unhurried' (Clark 2023) approach here in this experiential, sensory learning opportunity is key to him making sense of what is going on. The patterns of behaviour in his play demonstrate a mixture of enveloping and transporting schemas.

The outdoor world allows children to learn at their level and their pace, in a way that is less judgemental (Maynard & Waters, 2007). Moore (2015) suggests that when children acquire 'secret outdoor spaces', this can enable children to feel free, independent and 'not being watched' allows them to be more creative, engaging in activities and sometimes risks that require higher-level thinking. Opportunities that are afforded by being in an outdoor or natural environment can allow children to observe the effects of action on objects or materials (Athey 1990), in a way that is different to that of being in indoors. Outside, children have the space to engage in a deeper level of fantasy play and to develop positive dispositions for learning such as resilience, playfulness and reciprocity (Ouvry, 2003).

The outdoors can offer activities and resources on a larger scale because of the space available and having the space allows children to develop spatial awareness, as they are able to move themselves and larger objects around the space. Access to materials like sand and water, blocks, soil and wood not only provides a vast array of tactile materials but also encourages visual, olfactory, and auditory combinations to support learning. These sensory experiences are foundational to supporting the neural pathways in the brain that make connections when learning, and the outdoor environment heightens the senses enabling learning to percolate at a pace that works for the child and allows them to make sense of what is happening around them. As discussed in the previous chapter, Nature Pedagogy offers the opportunity to connect with the natural environment and is a powerful teaching and learning approach. It is where Loose parts play becomes a natural avenue for children to encounter, as they are given the freedom to explore their outdoor spaces and play in ways that enable them to be active, enhancing their senses and learning from each other, which provides the many benefits mentioned earlier in this chapter.

If we considered the outdoor spaces that children have access to, as equal in value to how indoor spaces support learning and development, then it could be recognised as a holistic approach to understanding how effective environments can support the development of schemas in young children. This aligns with Froebel's love of nature and the importance of affording children the opportunities to connect with living things in the outdoor environment. This work is well documented and suggests that the universal laws of nature such as gravity and motion, light and sound are best served by play in the outdoors and wider natural environment. Froebel believed that play was part of being human where the whole child is active, and how a child relates to their lived experiences (Tovey, 2020). Play is a fundamental vehicle for learning and Froebel envisioned the power of play as a place where children created deep connections and awareness, and where children made sense of the world around them (Froebel in Lilley, 1967). Froebelian principles propose that educators create long periods of uninterrupted, open-ended play…. where 'time is not filled' by the adult and children make links to different experiences, drawing on past experiences' (Tovey, 2017 in Clark 2023, p. 30), and when in nature they are allowed to 'venture' into wonder and creativity, making unusual connections (Boulton & Thomas, 2023). These opportunities provide strong cognitive dimensions to understanding how children make sense of the world and it is these repeated patterns of thinking that often manifest as schemas.

Where Does Risky Play Fit?

The concept of affordances as previously explained can account for the different forms of physical activity and the experiences provided by engaging with the materials and 'loose parts' that are available (Nedovic & Morrissey, 2013). However, research suggests a tension exists between what EY practitioners would like to provide for children and their 'accountability under regulations' (Sandseter, Wyver and Little, 2012, p. 307; Sandseter 2007; Sandseter 2009). Some regulations such as those suggested propose the removal of loose parts or moveable objects such as 'dangerous' sticks, large wooden structures and tyres, which would otherwise afford opportunities for construction (Johnson, 2013), and the development of schemas linked to transporting and enveloping, by creating 'undisturbed hiding places for play'. These opportunities are identified as essential chances for children to develop creativity, independence, and self-governance (Cobb-Moore & Miller, 2007; Moser & Martinsen, 2010).

Sandseter's research (2007) explored the debate still part of today's culture, of the balance between making sure our children are safe versus letting the children play in physically and emotionally stimulating and challenging environments. She categorised risky play into the six categories illustrated in Table 4.2, and each offers its own value to how children learn to regulate and assess risk whilst using a range of objects, tools and being afforded opportunities to be in natural spaces. It is apparent from these studies that many children are drawn to activities such as climbing, jumping from heights, sliding fast and balancing precariously. These experiences allow children to explore the limits of their abilities and to learn to assess and manage the risks involved (Christensen & Mikkelsen, 2008).

According to Ball (2004), exposure to injuries and sustaining minor injuries is a universal part of childhood through which children learn the consequences of their behaviour and understand their competencies and limitations. This ability to assess risk and weigh up the benefits against possible undesirable outcomes is an important life skill (Boyer, 2006). The opportunity for risk taking in play has been linked to positive developmental outcomes (Gill, 2007; Lavrysen et al., 2017). It is thought that the opportunity for risk taking improves children's competencies in risk management and risk perception. Consequently, the properties of different loose parts in the outdoors which may involve risky play, can afford children unique opportunities to develop and use their schemas.

Table 4.2 Sandseter's Categorisation of risky play (2007)

Categories	Risk	Sub-categories
A: Great heights	Danger of injury from falling	Climbing
		Jumping from still or flexible surfaces
		Balancing on high objects
		Hanging/swinging at great heights
B: High speed	Uncontrolled speed and pace that can lead to collision with something (or someone)	Swinging at high speed
		Slinging and sledging at high speed
		Running uncontrollably at high speed
		Bicycling at high speed
		Skating and skiing at high speed
C: Dangerous tool	Can lead to injuries and wounds	Cutting tools: knives, saws, axes
		Strangling tools: ropes etc.
D: Dangerous elements	Where children can fall into or form something	Cliffs
		Deep water or icy water
		Fire pits
E: Rough-and-tumble	Where the children can harm each other	Wresting
		Fencing with sticks, etc.
		Play fighting
F: Disappear/get lost	Where the children can disappear from the supervision of adults, get lost alone	Go exploring alone
		Playing alone in unfamiliar environments

Research Spotlight

Consider the article cited here:

Boulton, P., and Thomas, A. (2022a). How does play in the outdoors afford opportunities for schema development in young children? *International Journal of Play*, https://doi.org/10.1080/21594937.2022.2069348

For practitioners in ECE this paper may help to shed some light on the different types of dynamic schemas that we might expect to see in practice, but particularly how the affordances of the outdoor environment help children to construct knowledge and understanding. Practitioners' journeys are shared in how they came to understand schemas and how it shaped their pedagogy. Findings suggest that the use of the outdoors affords greater engagement of the senses, use of larger spaces and loose

Conclusion 53

parts, and it enables deeper learning where self-governance of the play underpins schematic development.

Reflect on the Article:

Now, consider the following questions in relation to your own experiences and practices:

1. How does your practice enable children to access the outdoors and loose parts play?
2. Using the audit, what loose parts and outdoor spaces do you have and how are they accessed and used by the children?
3. Does your understanding of schemas help you make connections to the behaviours that you observe in children's play?
4. Are the loose parts that you have meeting the needs of children?
5. What might you need to change?

Conclusion

This chapter has explored the ingredients that contribute to effective learning environments, particularly the outdoor environment as a valuable space for supporting children's schematic development. It has considered the theories of Loose parts and affordance and how they play critical roles in helping practitioners to see the world through the eyes of a child. The transformative play that can also occur 'in-between' the child and the Loose part has also been viewed through a relational materialist lens, where agency and intentionality are equally distributed between the 'players'. Understanding the unique ways that children perceive and use objects means that practitioners can plan and prepare to meet the learning and development needs of children in ways that can afford deep, sensory learning opportunities and where children can begin to assess their own risk and manage their play, whilst developing an understanding of the outdoor world around them.

Significant research into how children play underpins much of the discussion and influences what practitioners must debate as they consider their own pedagogies and the spaces they embrace, to offer children authentic experiences that have meaning. An opportunity is provided for you to review some research for yourself and then evaluate your own understanding and practice of using outdoor environments to nurture children's schemas. The outdoors is a space and place where children can learn at their own pace, where senses are heightened and affordance is rich, and play can occur 'in-between' the child and the object, enhancing meaning making. Outdoor spaces generate imagination beyond that assumed by an adult, it is where a tree branch can be a bridge, or a slide, or a tool to orientate/hang or suspend objects because that is how different children employ such a loose part in order to make sense of the world.

References

Ahn, S., & Fedewa, A. L. (2011). A meta-analysis of the relationship between children's physical activity and mental health. *Journal of Pediatric Psychology, 36*(4), 385–397. https://doi.org/10.1093/jpepsy/jsq107

Atherton, F. and Nutbrown, C. (2013). *Understanding Schemas and Young Children*. London: SAGE.

Athey, C. (1990). *Extending thought in young children: A parent–teacher partnership*. Paul Chapman.

Ball, D. J. (2004). Policy issues and risk-benefit trade-offs of "safer surfacing" for children's playgrounds. *Accident Analysis and Prevention, 36*, 661–670.

Bennett, J. (2010). *Vibrant matter: A political ecology of things*. Duke University Press.

Boulton, P., & Thomas, A. (2022a). How does play in the outdoors afford opportunities for schema development in young children? *International Journal of Play*. https://doi.org/10.1080/21594937.2022.2069348

Boulton, P., & Thomas, A. (2023). *Schemas, outdoor play and Froebel*. Available via: https://www.froebel.org.uk/news/schemas-outdoor-play-and-froebel. Accessed December 28th 2024.

Boyer, T. W. (2006). The development of risk-taking: A multi-perspective review. *Developmental Review, 26*, 291–345. Available via: https://doi.org/10.1016/j.dr.2006.05.002

Bundy, A., Luckett, T., Tranter, P., Naughton, G., Wyver, S., Ragen, J., & Spies, G. (2009). The risk is that there is "'no risk'": A simple, innovative intervention to increase children's activity levels. *International Journal of Early Years Education, 17*(1), 33–45. https://doi.org/10.1080/09669760802699878

Casey, T., & Robertson, J. (2019). *Loose parts play: A toolkit*. Edinburgh, Inspiring Scotland. Available via: https://www.playscotland.org/resources/print/Loose-Parts-Play-Tookit-Revised.pdf?plsctml_id=10924. Accessed January 31st 2025.

Christensen, P., & Mikkelsen, M. (2008). Jumping off and being careful: Children's strategies of risk management in everyday life. *Sociology of Health and Illness, 30*(1), 112–130. https://doi.org/10.1111/j.1467-9566.2007.01046.x

Clark, A. (2023). *Slow knowledge and the unhurried child*. Routledge.

Cobb-Moore, C., & Miller, M. (2007). Chapter 7: Contemporary Research in Childhood Education. In J. Ailwood (Ed.). *Early childhood in Australia—Historical and comparative contexts* (pp. 94–110). Australia: Pearson Education.

Dyment, J., & O'Connell, T. S. (2013). The impact of playground design on play choices and behaviors of pre-school children. *Children's Geographies, 11*(3), 263–280. https://doi.org/10.1080/14733285.2013.812272

Engelen, L., Bundy, A., Naughton, G., Simpson, J. M., Bauman, A., Ragen, J., Baur, L., Wyver, S., Tranter, P., Niehues, A., Schiller, W., Perry, G., Jessup, G., & van der Ploeg, H. P. (2013). Increasing physical activity in young primary school children it's child's play: A cluster randomised controlled trial. *Preventive Medicine, 56*(5), 319–325. https://doi.org/10.1016/j.ypmed.2013.02.007

Forman, G. (1994). Different media, different languages. In L. G. Katz & B. Cesarone (Eds.), *Reflections on the Reggio Emilia approach* (pp. 41–54). London: ERIC Clearinghouse on Elementary Early Childhood Education.

Frost, J. (1990). The early childhood playground. *Young Children, 45*(2), 81–82.

Gaver, W. (1991). *Technology Affordances*. In CHI '91. New Orleans. United States. [Conference or workshop item] doi: https://doi.org/10.1145/108844.10885610.1145/108844.108856.

Gibson, J. J. (1979). *The ecological approach to visual perception*. London: Houghton Mifflin.

Gibson, J. L., Cornell, M., & Gill, T. (2017). A systematic review of research into the impact of loose parts play on children's cognitive, social and emotional development. *School Mental Health, 9*, 295–309. https://doi.org/10.1007/s12310-017-9220-9

Gill, T. (2007). *No fear: Growing up in a risk averse society*. Calouste Gulbenkian Foundation.

References

Hobson, T. (2020). *Integrating Loose Parts Play in a Preschool Program*. Available via: https://edutopia.org/article/integrating-loose-parts-play-preschool-program?utm_content=linkpos5&utm_campaign=weekly-202-1-18&utm_source=edu-legacy&utm_medium=email. Accessed September 2024.

James, D. (2012). *Survey of the impact of Scrapstore PlayPod in primary schools*. Bristol: Children's Scrapstore.

Johnson, P. (2013). Schoolyard geographies: The influence of object-play and place-making on relationships. *Review of International Geographical Education, 3*(1), 77–92.

Lavrysen, A., Bertrands, E., Leyssen, L., Smets, L., Vanderspikken, A., & De Graef, P. (2017). Risky-play at school. Facilitating risk perception and competence in young children. *European Early Childhood Education Research Journal, 25*(1), 89–105.

Lester, S., Jones, O., & Russell, W. (2010). *Supporting school improvement through play: An evaluation of South Gloucestershire's outdoor play and learning programme*. Play England.

Lilley, I. (1967). *Friedrich Froebel. A selection of his writings*. Cambridge: Cambridge University Press.

Maynard, T., & Waters, J. (2007). Learning in the outdoor environment: A missed opportunity? *Journal of Early Years, 27*(3), 255–265.

Moser, T., & Martinsen, M. T. (2010). The outdoor environment in Norwegian Kindergartens as Pedagogical Spaces for Toddlers Play, learning and development. *European Early Childhood Education Research Journal, 18*(4), 457–471.

Moore, D. (2015). The teacher doesn't know what it is, but she knows where we are: Young children's secret places in early childhood outdoor environments. *International Journal of Play, 4*(1), 20–31.

Nedovic, S., & Morrissey, A. (2013). Calm active and focused: Children's responses to an organic outdoor learning environment. *Learning Environment Research, 16*, 281–295. https://doi.org/10.1007/s10984-013-9127-9

Nicholson, S. (1972). The theory of loose parts, an important principle for design methodology. *Studies in Design Education Craft & Technology*, 4(2). Retrieved from http://jil.lboro.ac.uk/ojs/index.php/SDEC/article/view/1204

Nutbrown, C. (2011). *Threads of thinking schemas and young children's learning* (4th ed.). Sage.

Ouvry, M. (2003). *Exercising muscles and minds*. London: National Children's Bureau.

Play Wales. (2017). *Resources for playing-providing loose parts to support children's play*. Play Wales: Cardiff.

Sandseter, E. B. H. (2007). Categorizing risky play—How can we identify risk-taking in children's play. *European Early Childhood Education Research Journal, 15*(2), 237–252. Available via: https://www.researchgate.net/publication/249047571_Categorising_risky_play-How_can_we_identify_risk-taking_in_children's_play#fullTextFileContent. Accessed January 2nd 2025.

Sandseter, E. B. H. (2009). Children's expressions of exhilaration and fear in risky play. *Contemporary issues in early childhood, 10*(2), 92–106.

Sandseter, E. B. H., Wyver, S., & Little, H. (2012). Does theory and pedagogy have an impact on provisions for outdoor learning? A comparrison of approaches in Australia and Norway. *Journal of Adventure Education and Outdoor Learning, 12*(3), 167–182.

Singh, A. (2012). Physical activity and performance at school. *Archives of Pediatrics and Adolescent Medicine, 166*(1), Article p49. https://doi.org/10.1001/archpediatrics.2011.716

Tovey, H. (2020). *Froebel's principles and practcie today*. Froebel Trust. Available via: https://froebel.org.uk/training-and-resources/pamphlets. Accessed October 2024.

Taguchi, H. L. (2011). Investigating learning, participation and becoming in early childhood practices with a relational materialist approach. *Global Studies of Childhood, 1*(1), 36–50.

Welsh Government (WG). (2020a). *Curriculum for Wales Guidance*. Cardiff: Crown Copyright.

Welsh Government (WG). (2022a). *A curriculum for funded non-maintained nursery settings*. Available via: https://hwb.gov.wales/api/storage/b1801d78-38c3-4320-9818-d9996c21aef8/220914-a-curriculum-for-funded-non-maintained-nursery-settings.pdf. Accessed 31 October 2023.

White, J. (2013). *Playing and learning outdoors: Making provision for high quality experiences in the outdoor environment with children 3–7*. Routledge.

Chapter 5
Rotational Schema and Loose Parts

Definition A dynamic rotational schema can be defined as 'turning, twisting or rolling oneself or objects around' (Arnold and the Pen Green Team, 2010).

Rotational Schema in Action

Emily is 3 years old in these photos. She has been attending the nursery on a regular basis. The nursery has been making Easter bonnets and Emily has been fascinated with creating her own hat. She has taken a bowl of pipe cleaners and a sieve from the Kitchen area to work with. In these photos, Emily did not explore the sieve in the usual way. She wanted to explore the holes, so she turned the sieve upside down and then twisted several pipe cleaners into the holes. She repeated this until she was happy and then she proudly held up the upside-down sieve to show off her work. Emily said, '*Look it's my Easter hat, it's really lovely*'—the setting had been making Easter bonnets that week. Here Emily can be considered to be using the 'thought (internalized data and telling a story)' category (Athey 1990, p. 116). Here the pipe cleaners can be considered the loose parts (Figs. 5.1, 5.2).

Nutbrown (2011) evidenced that children with a dynamic circular schema explored rotation and roundness. Here Emily is exploring the roundness of the holes in the sieve and how the round pipe cleaners can fit inside the round holes. Emily has taken the idea of an Easter bonnet and used her rotational schema to explore how the sieve and pipe cleaners can be used to represent her own version. Emily is at the pre-operational stage of cognitive development, and she is 'explaining … knowledge through understanding' (England, p. 7).

In Fig. 5.3, Toby is twisting the sieve down into the sand to make it come up through the holes before pouring the sand through the sieve in the traditional way. He seemed surprised to see the sand come up through the sieve and exclaimed, '*Look it's pushing up the holes, look*'. In Fig. 5.4, Toby is watching the sand fall through the

Fig. 5.1 Twisting pipe cleaners to go through the sieve

Fig. 5.2 Feeling chuffed with the result

bottom of the sieve and back into the sand tray. As Toby seemed surprised by this, it could be argued that he did not expect this to happen, and he was assimilating new information (the sand being forced up into the sieve) and needed to accommodate his understanding to take account of this new development (Piaget, 1953). He then repeated this action to reinforce this understanding. This could be an example of what Piaget meant by disequilibrium, where thinking needed to be adjusted to take account of a new (or surprising) development (Piaget 1954). Here we can also consider the relational materialist approach (Taguchi 2011) where we consider how the sand plays with Toby as well as vice versa. The play is taking place 'in-between' the sand and the sieve [loose parts] and Toby and there is no hierarchy between them in the play. The physical forces applied between Toby and the sand as he pushes and pours the sand, and as the sand pushes back and falls through the holes, overlap into each other and thus agency and intentionality are distributed between them; this is where the sand affords Toby a unique sensory learning opportunity to make meaning of what is happening and as this occurs a process of transformation takes place.

This episode with Toby reinforces the need for close observation along with a knowledge of schemas as otherwise this could have easily been missed. This is

Fig. 5.3 Twisting the sieve down into the sand to make it come up through the holes

Fig. 5.4 Pouring sand into the sieve to fall through the holes

where an attuned adult when viewing Toby's actions through a schematic lens can support his new knowledge and understanding by providing other opportunities for him to learn about downward forces and upward thrust.

In all these images, the children are exploring the roundness of holes and how different media can be put through these holes. In Figs. 5.1 and 5.2, Emily is investigating how the pipe cleaners can be twisted to go through the holes on the bottom of the sieve. Toby is exploring how sand can go upwards through the holes in the sieve (Fig. 5.3). Both children are repeating these actions and as Conkbayir (2017) argues '…repetition is considered to be an essential influence in promoting neural growth'.

Rotational Schema and Loose Parts in the Outdoors

As discussed in Chapter 4, loose parts play can be resources and materials that facilitate open-ended play. Here the pipe cleaners and the sand are loose parts as they can be used in several ways and for these children, both resources have allowed them to explore the roundness of their rotational schema. Further as also detailed in Chapter 4, the pipe cleaners and sand have affordances that allow them to be manipulated in different ways, again nurturing the children's rotational schema.

Toby believed that it was the sand pushing up the holes in the sieve and did not understand that it was the force of the sieve being pushed and twisted down into the sand that forced the sand up through the holes. This is where the theories of affordance and loose parts blend to foster creativity and experimentation and where Toby and the sand work collaboratively, as one action cannot exist without the other, thus transformative learning occurs. Here is an opportunity for an attuned practitioner to become a play partner with Toby and to explain this concept. Piaget (1959, p. 263) asserted that developing 'dialogue' with a child allows the adult to gain a window into their world and to work with them to develop their knowledge and understanding. However, to have these meaningful conversations there needs to be careful observations with the children and Broadhead urged practitioners to move away from simply watching children to 'thinking and talking about their learning' (2004, p. 131).

Other loose parts that can be associated with rotational schemas might be objects such as tyres, hula hoops, rolls of string and kitchen whisks in water, and painting with water. As previously explained objects' affordances will be unique to different children, and they will see rotation in objects that are not always viewed in that way by the adult. This is why thinking and talking about what we observe in children's play is so important, to make sense of what we observe. Being outdoors means that these sorts of loose parts have more space to be moved and used in ways that could not occur indoors and can result in children developing greater physical skills as well as working collaboratively—e.g. rolling the tyre together due to its size/weight, one child unrolling the string, whilst the other rolls it back up. Children who engage with repeated play patterns of whisking water or painting circles with water on the ground or often on wood in the outdoor play area can also be indicative of rotational schemas. When play is messy outdoors, it engages the senses, heightening the learning and its ability to be assimilated.

Rotational Schemas and the Four Operating Levels

As discussed in Chapter 2, Piaget (1962) described schema as operating at four levels, which Athey (1990, 2007) then exemplified in her research. If we look at the images in this chapter depicting a rotational schema in terms of the four levels, then we can see the following:

At a motor level, both Emily and Toby are using their actions to twist the pipe cleaners into the holes of the sieve repeatedly and twist the sieve downwards into the sand. Both Emily and Toby are assimilating new information on how the pipe cleaners and sand behave (Piaget, 1953).

At a symbolic level, Emily has stated that the pipe cleaners and sieve are her 'Easter Hat'. So, she is using symbols and language to discuss her activities. Toby has not indicated any symbolism with the sand and the sieve, but he has used language to express his surprise at the sand coming up through the holes.

Both children are using functional dependency as Emily has worked out that the pipe cleaners need to be twisted to go through the holes to make a pattern on the bottom of the sieve. Toby has worked out that you must push and twist the sieve into the sand to make the sand come up through the holes.

Atherton and Nutbrown (2013), Nutbrown (2011) and Athey (2007) all agree that sensory and perceptual information alongside motor-level actions leads to higher-level understanding. Here Emily and Toby have felt the force needed to twist the pipe cleaners into place and the force needed to twist the sieve downwards into the sand.

At the thought level, Emily can create her own Easter hat by recalling what they look like from previous experience. In the Froebel project, Athey (1990) proposed that thought was indicated when children could recall experiences without a concrete reminder of the event and she postulated that there is a match between 'forms of thought and appropriate speech' (1990, p. 164). Emily was able to articulate what she was doing whilst pushing the pipe cleaners through the sieve.

Curriculum Links

In terms of curriculum links, examples can be seen in the toolkit for the Curriculum for Funded Non-maintained Nursery Settings (Boulton & Thomas, 2022b) and applied to practice, and the following ideas and information from the schema toolkit can be used (Figs. 5.5, 5.6):

The full toolkit can be downloaded from: https://hwb.gov.wales/repository/resource/39397e24-d5e9-4b57-ad15-09f64f4ad0ec/overview

Taking the Learning Forward

If we consider Emily and Toby, then in terms of the non-maintained curriculum developmental pathways in Wales, the wellbeing pathway is evident as both children are following their interests, and the adults are valuing their play. Both children are developing their fine motor skills through threading pipe cleaners and twisting the sieve into the sand. Their curiosity is being supported by adults in the setting giving

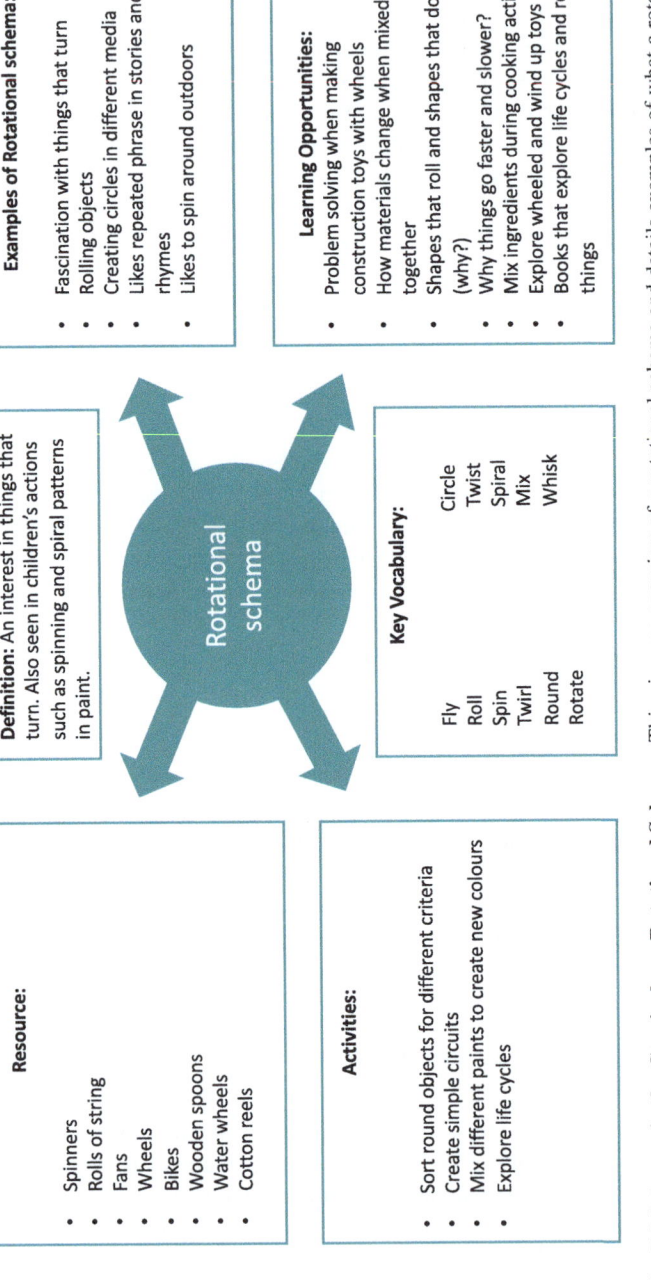

Fig. 5.5 **Schemas in the Curriculum: Rotational Schema** This gives an overview of a rotational schema and details examples of what a rotational schema looks like in practice and planned activities, resources and vocabulary that can support a rotational schema

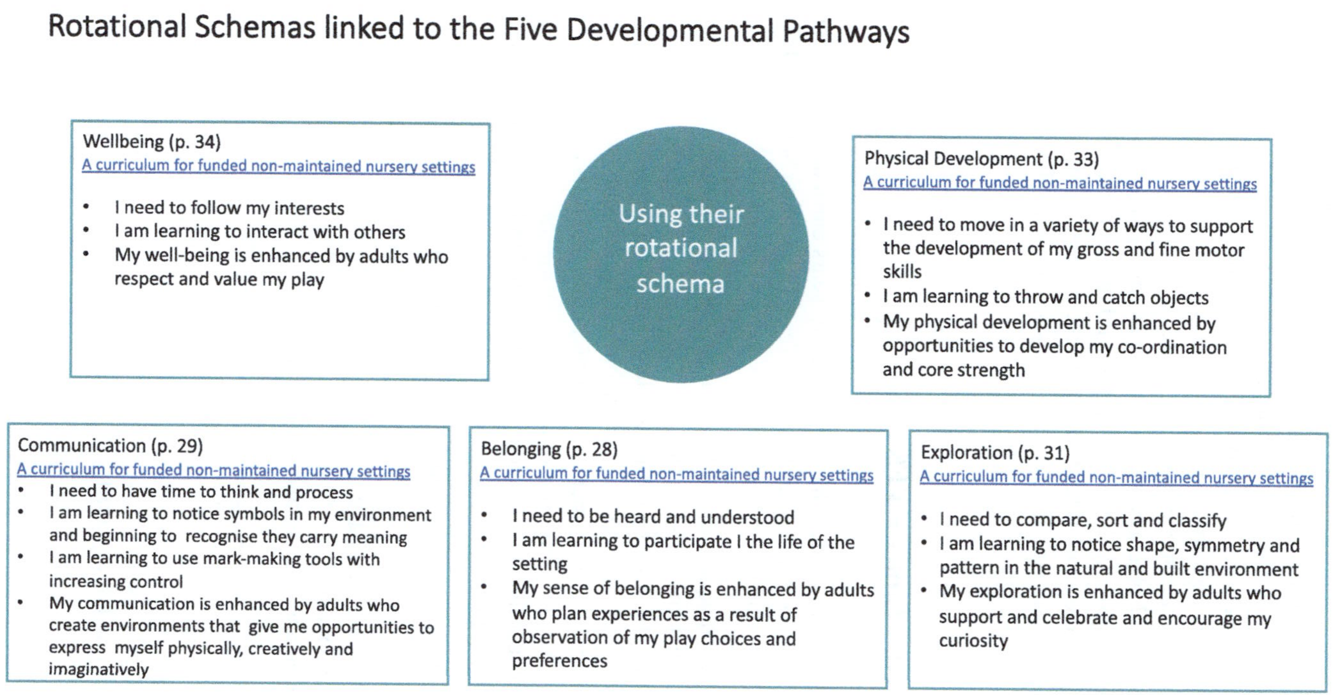

Rotational Schemas linked to the Five Developmental Pathways

Wellbeing (p. 34)
A curriculum for funded non-maintained nursery settings
- I need to follow my interests
- I am learning to interact with others
- My well-being is enhanced by adults who respect and value my play

Communication (p. 29)
A curriculum for funded non-maintained nursery settings
- I need to have time to think and process
- I am learning to notice symbols in my environment and beginning to recognise they carry meaning
- I am learning to use mark-making tools with increasing control
- My communication is enhanced by adults who create environments that give me opportunities to express myself physically, creatively and imaginatively

Using their rotational schema

Physical Development (p. 33)
A curriculum for funded non-maintained nursery settings
- I need to move in a variety of ways to support the development of my gross and fine motor skills
- I am learning to throw and catch objects
- My physical development is enhanced by opportunities to develop my co-ordination and core strength

Belonging (p. 28)
A curriculum for funded non-maintained nursery settings
- I need to be heard and understood
- I am learning to participate I the life of the setting
- My sense of belonging is enhanced by adults who plan experiences as a result of observation of my play choices and preferences

Exploration (p. 31)
A curriculum for funded non-maintained nursery settings
- I need to compare, sort and classify
- I am learning to notice shape, symmetry and pattern in the natural and built environment
- My exploration is enhanced by adults who support and celebrate and encourage my curiosity

Fig. 5.6 Rotational Schema & the five developmental pathways This shows how a rotational schema can support a child's development through the five developmental pathways (Boulton & Thomas, 2022b)

them time and space to play with the pipe cleaners and the sand. Both children are having their communication skills met by adults who are encouraging their creativity.

For Toby, the opportunity to use outdoor spaces enables him to engage with loose parts that require more space and are likely to be messy. As a result, the play encourages Toby to use forces and flows that nurture physical development and he uses the resources in ways that evoke a response from the materials he is using. Moving this forward in practice, providing Toby with more space e.g. an outdoor sand pit and additional objects/containers such as jugs, colanders and if possible, introducing a pulley system/wheels and cogs would further nurture his development. These loose parts would support his rotational schema development, where the sand can be transported by using rotational movements/actions, extending his development cognitively and physically.

Other Curricula Links-EYFS

As briefly mentioned in earlier chapters, the early years curriculum in England for children aged 0–5 years is known as the Early Years Foundation Stage (EYFS). This curriculum has four guiding principles which are:

- Every child is a unique child, who is constantly learning and can be resilient, capable, confident and self-assured.
- Children learn to be strong and independent through positive relationships.
- Children learn and develop well in enabling environments with teaching and support from adults, who respond to their individual interests and needs and help them to build their learning over time.
- Importance of learning and development. Children develop and learn at different rates (DfE, 2024, p. 7).

There are seven areas of learning and development which are divided into three Prime areas:

- Communication and language
- Physical development
- Personal, social and emotional development

And four specific areas:

- Literacy
- Mathematics
- Understanding the world
- Expressive arts and design (DfE, 2024)

There are the early learning goals (ELG) children are expected to reach by the time they leave the EYFS at the age of 5 years and there are ELG for each of the seven areas of learning and development.

If we look at the schematic actions of Emily and Toby through an EYFS lens, then we can see the following. In terms of communication and language, they are meeting the following ELG for Speaking:

'Express their ideas and feelings about their experiences using full sentences, including use of past, present and future tenses and making use of conjunctions, with modelling and support from their teacher' (DfE, 2024, p. 12). Both Emily and Toby are stating what they are doing. Emily is able to recall an experience she has had with making an Easter bonnet. Toby is able to voice his surprise with the sand coming up into the sieve.

For the ELG for Personal, Social and Emotional Development, the following applies:

'Be confident to try new activities and show independence, resilience and perseverance in the face of challenge' (DfE, 2024, p. 13). Both children have persevered with their activities. Emily has spent time twisting pipe cleaners through a sieve and Toby has spent time twisting sand up into a sieve.

For the ELG for Expressive Arts and Design Emily and Toby can:

'Safely use and explore a variety of materials, tools and techniques, experimenting with colour, design, texture, form and function' (DfE, 2024, p. 15). Both children are using materials and tools that support their rotational schema and are experimenting.

In addition to the EYFS curriculum document, there is the Development Matters guidance (DfE, 2023). Here practitioners are encouraged to recognise that young children's learning is often driven by their interests and that plans need to be flexible (DfE, 2023). This is evident in the photographs of both Emily and Toby. The practitioners have not told Emily that she cannot take the sieve from the kitchen area to use. The guidance goes on further to explain that there are three important characteristics of effective pedagogy which are:

- playing and exploring—children investigate and experience things, and 'have a go'
- active learning—children concentrate and keep on trying if they encounter difficulties, and enjoy achievements
- creating and thinking critically—children have and develop their own ideas, make links between ideas and develop strategies for doing things

Through nurturing children's rotational schemas, they can be seen to be investigating, being active learners and they are creating and thinking critically. Toby has learnt that if he uses a force to twist down on a material like sand, it will be pushed up through the sieve's holes. Emily has learned that if she twists pipe cleaners through a sieve, she can create a representation of an Easter bonnet. The guidance refers to children bringing their own interests and fascinations into a setting and this will nurture their learning. Schemas are predicated on a child's interests and fascinations. The role of the adult is to nurture and nourish these schemas and to provide a learning environment both indoors and outdoors which includes stimulating loose parts for them to access easily.

For both Toby and Emily there are opportunities for the practitioners working with them to extend their learning by exploring forces, different surface areas that allow objects to roll across them, and exploring different-sized objects that will only fit through certain-sized holes. However, unless practitioners are familiar with schemas and can observe children carefully. These learning opportunities can be missed. Remember the observation cycle in Chapter 2 (Figs. 5.7, 5.8):

Fig. 5.7 The observation Cycle (WG, 2023a)

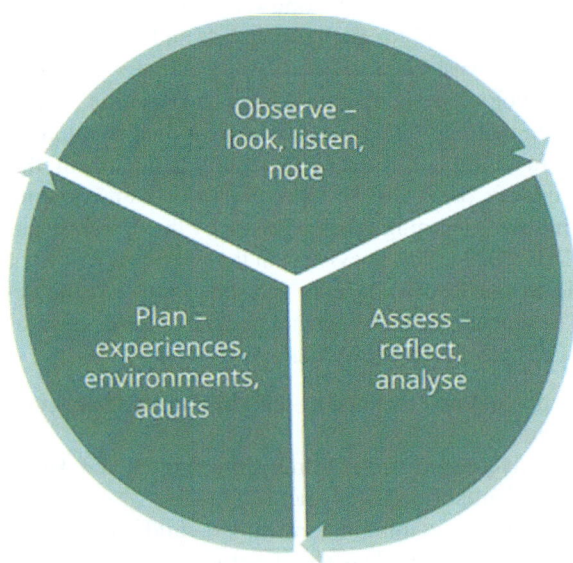

Other Curricula Links-EYFS

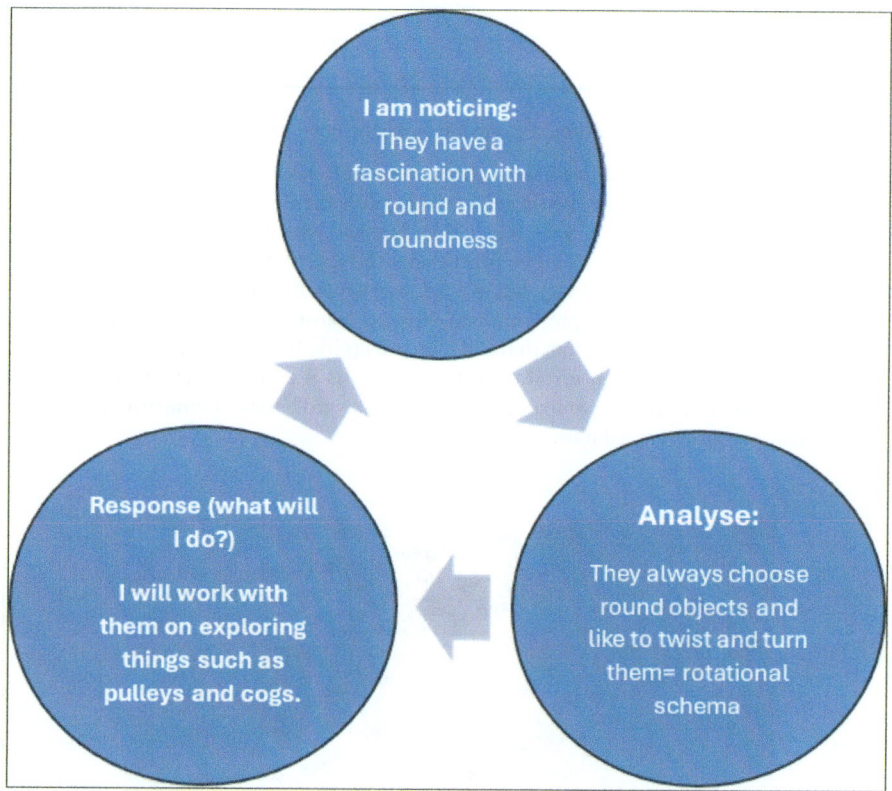

Fig. 5.8 Using the observation cycle for Toby and Emily

If we look at Toby and Emily's actions and use the observation cycle, then we can have the following:

Recipe

Case Study: Today the children are outside and have been given a range of PE equipment to play with. Toby immediately chooses the hula hoop. However, he does not use it in the traditional way, but instead starts to roll the hoop over the rope bridge repeatedly back and fro (Fig. 5.9). When Toby is asked what he is doing he replies, '*I am taking the hoop for a walk*'. The practitioner did not try to persuade Toby to use the hoop in a more traditional way, but instead, was happy to allow Toby to explore the roundness of the hoop in his preferred way. Toby is learning about size-can the hoop fit in this space and is there room to roll it? He is learning how it feels to roll the hoop over different surfaces. Can it roll over this surface, is it easier or harder to roll the hoop over the rope surface compared to the concrete yard? Toby continues to roll the hoop around yard for the duration of the playtime.

Fig. 5.9 Rolling a hoop across the bridge

Here Toby is learning about how the hoop feels when it rolls over different surfaces. He is experimenting in how he can get the hoop to roll over a rope surface that has gaps. This will feel very different to how the hoop will feel on a hard surface like the playground. Again, Toby is exploring force as with the sieve pushed downwards into the sand, however, he will use a different amount of force to enable the hoop to roll over the rope bridge to rolling the hoop over the tarmac of the playground. He will

> learn about the reciprocal forces as reactions to different surfaces and he will begin to learn that different materials have agency and respond in different ways.

Questions to Consider:

1. Using the toolkit, how could you consider meeting Toby's need to use his rotational schema in a variety of ways?
2. Can you think of any children you work with that have a rotational schema and what resources do you provide to support it?
3. As an attuned adult, how would you facilitate Toby in using the hula hoop in a different way?

Conclusion

This chapter has defined what is meant by a rotational schema and how it can be observed in practice. It has explored how different loose parts in both indoors and outdoors can nurture and nourish a rotational schema. It has highlighted how attuned practitioners can provide resources and the time and space for children to explore their rotational schemas and reminded us of the importance of thinking and talking about what we observe in children's play because what the adult perceives is not always how children think about their environment or how they use the objects available to them. Once observed, practitioners can use the toolkit to provide a range of resources that can allow children to discover new ways of learning through their rotational schema. For example, Emily has worked out how to fit pipe cleaners through the round holes of the sieve to create her own Easter bonnet. Toby has discovered how twisting a sieve downwards into sand forces the sand up through the round holes of the sieve. We have also considered how messy play outdoors and natural materials can support holistic development and afford opportunities for children to explore their rotational schemas, as their senses are heightened, and learning is often deeper as a consequence. There has been a consideration of how a rotational schema can support children's development in the EYFS. There has been an exploration of the ELG and how these can be met by supporting children's rotational schemas in a supportive learning environment with enabling adults.

There have been questions to consider and a case study to reflect upon. This chapter has shown how loose parts both indoors and outdoors can afford children the opportunities to explore their rotational schema.

Reflective Questions:

1. Having read this chapter, can you think of any children you know that have a rotational schema?
2. Can you think of ways you or your setting can support a child's rotational schema? Use the toolkit to help you.

Key Takeaways: A List of the Main Schematic Features of a Rotational Schema

1. **Spinning Objects**—Children enjoy spinning toys, wheels, tops or other objects.
2. **Body Rotation**—Repeated movements such as twirling, rolling or spinning themselves around.
3. **Drawing Circles and Spirals**—A preference for creating circular patterns in drawings or scribbles.
4. **Turning and Twisting**—Engaging in actions like twisting lids, turning knobs or winding up toys.
5. **Observing Rotations**—A fascination with watching rotating objects, such as washing machines, fans or rolling balls.
6. **Movement Around Axes**—Running in circles, cycling or using playground equipment like merry-go-rounds.
7. **Interest in Circular Motion in Play**—Enjoying activities that involve swirling water, stirring mixtures or rolling balls.
8. **Developmental Significance**—Helps children develop coordination, spatial awareness and an understanding of physics concepts like rotation and force.

Opportunities for Further Reading

- Louis S (2021) Schemas for Parents. Available via: https://kidsdawntildusk.co.uk/wp-content/uploads/2022/05/1473170200_SchemasforParentsBooklet2021.pdf

References

Arnold C and The Pen Green Team. (2010). *Understanding schemas and emotion.* SAGE.

Atherton, F., & Nutbrown, C. (2013). *Understanding schemas and young children.* Sage.

Athey, C. (1990). *Extending Thought in Young Children: A Parent-Teacher Partnership.* London: Paul Chapman.

Athey, C. (2007). *Extending thought in young children: A parent–teacher partnership* (2nd ed.). Sage.

Boulton, P., & Thomas, A. (2022b). *Schematic development and the curriculum for funded non-maintained nursery settings toolkit.* Available via: https://hwb.gov.wales/repository/resource/39397e24-d5e9-4b57-ad15-09f64f4ad0ec/en/overview. Accessed 23rd October 2024.

Broadhead, P. (2004). *Early years play and learning: Developing social skills and co-operation.* Routledge Falmer.

Conkbayir, M. (2017) *Early childhood and neuroscience: Theory, research and implications for practice.* London: Bloomsbury Publishing.

Department for Education (DfE). (2023). *Development matters.* Available via: https://assets.publishing.service.gov.uk/media/64e6002a20ae890014f26cbc/DfE_Development_Matters_Report_Sep2023.pdf. Accessed 30th November 2024.

References

Department for Education (DfE). (2024). *Early years foundation stage statutory framework*. Available via: https://assets.publishing.service.gov.uk/media/68c024cb8c6d992f23edd79c/Early_years_foundation_stage_statutory_framework_-_for_group_and_school-based_providers.pdf.pdf. Accessed 30th November 2024.

Nutbrown, C. (2011). *Threads of thinking schemas and young children's learning* (4th ed.). SAGE.

Piaget, J. (1953). *The origins of intelligence in the child* (2nd ed.). Routledge and Kegan Paul.

Piaget, J. (1954) *The construction of reality in the child*. New York: Basic Books.

Piaget, J. (1959). *The language and thought of the child*. Routledge and Kegan Paul.

Piaget, J. (1962). *Play, dreams and imitation in childhood*. London: Routledge and Kegan Paul.

Taguchi, H. L. (2011). Investigating learning participation and becoming in early childhood practices with a relational materialist approach. *Global Studies of Childhood., 1*(1), 36–50.

Welsh Government (WG). (2023a). *Observation*. Available via: View—Hwb (gov.wales). Accessed 01 December 2023.

Chapter 6
Trajectory Schema and Loose Parts

Definition A dynamic trajectory schema can be defined as an interest in dropping things…or climbing up and jumping off things (Louis et al., 2008) (Figs. 6.1, 6.2).

Trajectory Schema in Action

In these images, the children are exploring their vertical trajectory schemas. Both children have used loose parts inside and outside to build a tower. George spent a lot of time concentrating in getting each block in the right place so it would not fall over. Ellis was more concerned in making sure the tower was taller than him, even if it meant standing on tip toes to put the last block on.

Once the towers were built, both boys stood back and admired their work. The practitioner asked them if they were pleased with their towers and both boys said yes, with George jumping up and down on the spot to show his sense of happiness. Ellis was keen to explain that the tower was taller than him and *'nearly reached the sky'*.

Mairs and the Pen Green Team (2013) have described the importance of a supportive environment where children can explore their 'own fascinations' and 'develop mastery' (p. 141). Both children were given time and space to explore how the blocks could be used to build the vertical towers. The children knew that they could play with the blocks uninterruptedly in both indoors and outdoors, and that the practitioners would be supportive in allowing them free rein to use the blocks for their towers.

Fig. 6.1 George building a vertical tower indoors

Fig. 6.2 Ellis using loose parts to build a vertical tower outdoors

Trajectory Schema and Loose Parts in the Outdoors

With a fascination and personal interest in nature and the environment, when observing children in outdoor spaces it has often revealed connections between how they learn and how the features of the environment can stimulate and develop their understanding. It's how 'affordance' (Gibson 1979) works as explained in Chapter 4. How a child engages with that feature will be unique and will depend on their abilities, which change over time. Trajectory schemas can be horizontal and vertical and outdoor spaces can effectively support both where the child operates, exploring movement with their own body as well as perhaps moving objects through that space.

A dynamic horizontal trajectory can be explored through movement in curves, arcs or lines. Opportunities through designing outdoor spaces and gardens lend itself to the skills of landscape architects who consider the positionality of paths to be influential in how people especially children use and engage with outdoor spaces (Strinste, 2019). Paths in lines encourage movement and travel but also extend beyond the physical and bring new meaning to vocabulary which can be introduced by the practitioner, such as, follow, over there, here, along, across as well as many other actions and interpretations of movement which are bigger and much more sensory when in the outdoors. The amount of space that being outside affords enables aspects of 'direction' and 'routes' to be explored too and this fosters the concept of journeys and adventures. Taking objects along for the journey encourages children to use imagination and so the horizontal trajectory can become an adventure. Garden paths and nature trails draw children in, and they are compelled to respond to them (Wilenski & Wending, 2013).

Similarly, in the same vein, the dynamic vertical trajectory can be considered in outside spaces, and the topography of the space can offer a range of opportunities for children to repeat their 'up and down patterns' of behaviour. In relation to the landscape and what it offers, features such as slopes, steps, platforms, trees/tree stumps and bridges allow children to explore being 'high up' and 'low down', have different viewpoints and develop spatial awareness, as well as height and distance. In addition, natural materials like water, sand and soil are substances that move and have their own agency in terms of texture, structure and ability to flow as well as to be contained. Using materials such as these outdoors, where more space is afforded to children, enables them to use the natural materials in ways that may be messy but also move them using methods that align to a schema. For example, pouring from a height from one container to another or from their hands to a bucket offers a sensory experience where the child and the material actively engage with each other and the forces and flow form an assemblage that emerges as interactions between them (Taguchi 2011), nurturing the schema. Children can explore the notions of speed, direction and experiment with different quantities and spaces. So, it is important to consider a wide range of Loose parts and features that can offer these sensations and perspectives.for children who demonstrate repeated patterns of behaviour, which can be used to align with their trajectory schemas.

Trajectory Schemas and the Four Operating Levels

If we look at the images in this chapter depicting a trajectory schema in terms of the four levels, then we can see the following:

At a motor level, both George and Ellis are using their actions to build their towers. They are assimilating which blocks will sit on each other to build a stable foundation for their towers.

At a symbolic level, both have stated that the blocks represent a tower. Both children are using functional dependency as they are working out which blocks are best to fit on top of each other.

Both are developing their thinking as they are building towers without a concrete reminder of what a tower looks like. Louis et al., (2008) defines the development of thought as children using 'prior knowledge in their interaction with people, experiences and materials (p. 16).

Curriculum Links

In terms of curriculum links using the toolkit for Non-maintained Nursery Settings (Boulton & Thomas, 2022b) then the following can be used (Figs. 6.3, 6.4):

The full toolkit can be downloaded from: https://hwb.gov.wales/repository/resource/39397e24-d5e9-4b57-ad15-09f64f4ad0ec/overview

Curriculum Links

Schemas in the curriculum for non-maintained nursery settings: Trajectory schema

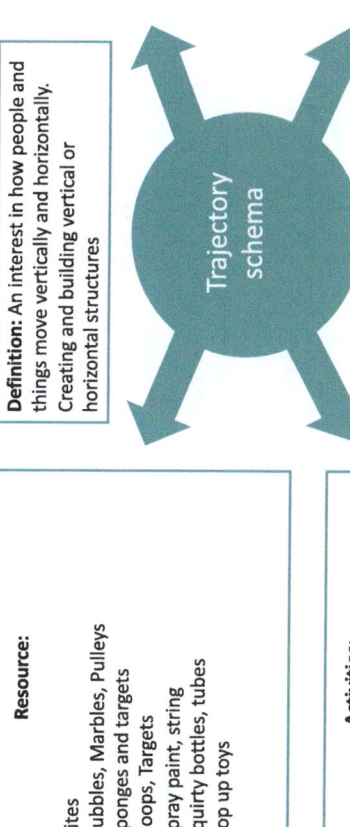

Resource:
- Kites
- Bubbles, Marbles, Pulleys
- Sponges and targets
- Hoops, Targets
- Spray paint, string
- Squirty bottles, tubes
- Pop up toys

Definition: An interest in how people and things move vertically and horizontally. Creating and building vertical or horizontal structures

Examples of Trajectory schema
- Dropping objects from different heights
- Climbing up and down repeatedly
- Throwing objects
- Rolling objects
- Bouncing objects
- Pressing buttons continually
- Stacking objects

Activities:
- Children to problem solve how to make something go faster/slower
- Construct own moving model
- Sort objects based on pushing and pulling
- Measure heights and distances
- Explore body movements in straight and oblique lines

Key Vocabulary:
Fly, spin   Fall
Drop, float   Twirl
Heavy, light   Swing, pulley
Up, down, fast
Land, target, take off
Slow, high, low, bounce

Learning Opportunities:
- Investigate how objects move
- Understand different directions
- Different lengths of objects and heights
- Introduce the concept of faster and slower
- Design vertical and horizontal structures
- Number lines to count objects

Fig. 6.3 Schemas in the curriculum: Trajectory schemas This gives an overview of a trajectory schema and details examples of what a trajectory schema looks like in practice and planned activities, resources and vocabulary that can support a trajectory schema

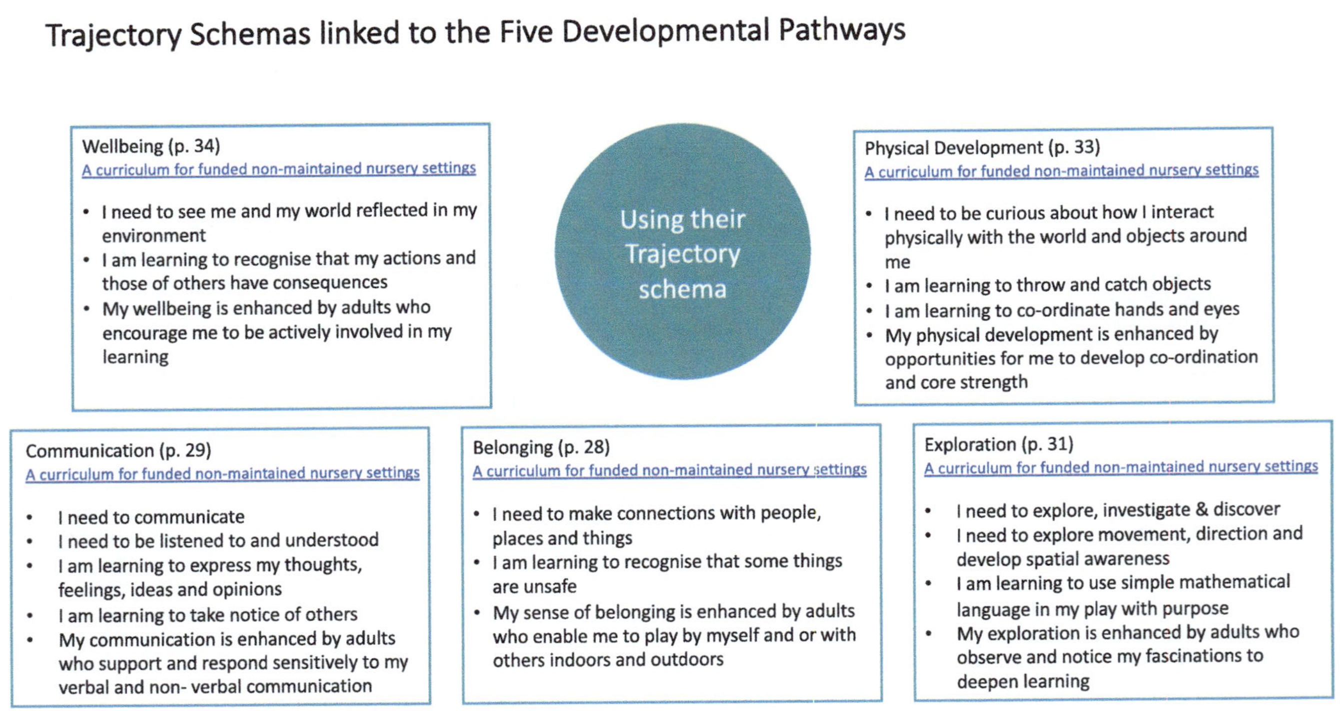

Trajectory Schemas linked to the Five Developmental Pathways

Wellbeing (p. 34)
A curriculum for funded non-maintained nursery settings

- I need to see me and my world reflected in my environment
- I am learning to recognise that my actions and those of others have consequences
- My wellbeing is enhanced by adults who encourage me to be actively involved in my learning

Communication (p. 29)
A curriculum for funded non-maintained nursery settings

- I need to communicate
- I need to be listened to and understood
- I am learning to express my thoughts, feelings, ideas and opinions
- I am learning to take notice of others
- My communication is enhanced by adults who support and respond sensitively to my verbal and non-verbal communication

Physical Development (p. 33)
A curriculum for funded non-maintained nursery settings

- I need to be curious about how I interact physically with the world and objects around me
- I am learning to throw and catch objects
- I am learning to co-ordinate hands and eyes
- My physical development is enhanced by opportunities for me to develop co-ordination and core strength

Belonging (p. 28)
A curriculum for funded non-maintained nursery settings

- I need to make connections with people, places and things
- I am learning to recognise that some things are unsafe
- My sense of belonging is enhanced by adults who enable me to play by myself and or with others indoors and outdoors

Exploration (p. 31)
A curriculum for funded non-maintained nursery settings

- I need to explore, investigate & discover
- I need to explore movement, direction and develop spatial awareness
- I am learning to use simple mathematical language in my play with purpose
- My exploration is enhanced by adults who observe and notice my fascinations to deepen learning

Using their Trajectory schema

Fig. 6.4 Trajectory schema & the five developmental pathways This shows how a trajectory schema can support a child's development through the five pathways

Taking the Learning Forward

For both George and Ellis there are opportunities for the practitioners working with them to extend their learning by exploring other building materials and exploring materials that move in a horizontal fashion like balls through a drainpipe, or marbles to nurture horizontal trajectories. Perhaps setting up target games such as getting a bean bag into a hoop or bucket could be useful to support a dynamic horizontal trajectory and the use of pulleys will help with direction and how objects move. However, unless practitioners are familiar with schemas and can observe children carefully. These learning opportunities can be missed.

In Fig. 6.2 Ellis's developmental pathways are being nurtured through his play and his **wellbeing** is considered as he is encouraged by the adults to be actively involved in his learning as he was given time and space to **explore,** which enables him to develop an understanding of the concepts of movement, spatial awareness and direction. Adults in this setting recognise and notice that Ellis has a fascination with height and building things up and in doing so they support his **physical development** through balance and strength, by giving him agency to move and 'build' as he chooses using the loose parts. **Communication** is also a key aspect of the learning taking place and vocabulary in this activity includes 'up there', 'down here', 'on top', 'underneath', 'in between' and descriptions of measurement such as 'too big', 'too heavy', 'as big as …'. Materials that can be manipulated, changed and moved feed a child's developmental needs (Nicolson & Shipstead, 2002).

Other Curricula Links: Realising the Ambition-Being Me in Scotland

In Scotland, there is a framework for children from early years to primary school age. It looks at the child as an individual, the importance of the environment (to include interactions, experiences and spaces) and the culture surrounding the child (Education Scotland, 2020). There are three themes underpinning this framework: wellbeing (including self, social, emotional and communication), movement and coordination, confidence, creativity and curiosity. If we look at wellbeing, then supporting a child's trajectory schema will facilitate the child to 'experience stimulating and challenging play spaces outdoors and in' (Education Scotland, 2020, p. 27). Both boys are using play space indoors and outdoors to build vertical towers that support their trajectory schema.

For movement, the document makes the following reference to schemas', I need you to understand and observe that I often repeat movements to make sense of experiences and develop my skills (schemas)' (Education Scotland, 2020, p. 28). In this chapter, the boys have been observed to repeatedly build towers with different resources and in different spaces. The framework goes on to state that children need, 'Access to resources that encourage open-ended experimentation which helps develop my fine and gross motor skills. For example, loose parts play can involve large blocks I need to physically manipulate or small parts I need to carefully select and place on an artwork I am creating' (Education Scotland, 2020, p. 28). Here the loose parts are the blocks that are facilitating the boys' knowledge and understanding of height and stability. The adults are encouraged to, 'Carefully observe my play to know when best to stand back, give me time, and allow me to investigate for myself—and notice the moments when I'm receptive to more support' (Education Scotland, 2020, p. 30). The adults have already observed the boys' repeated actions linked to a trajectory schema, so they are attuned to their way of learning. They have allowed the boys the time and space to build their towers, only helping if needed. Page 30 of the framework states the following, 'In all experiences notice and encourage my schematic play—through the process of my repeated actions I am learning about my world and how things work'. Pages 34–36 detail different types of schemas and how they can be supported. The framework also espouses the importance of play and the affordance of having experiences both indoors and outdoors, and adults observing the children to notice their play preferences, etc. (Education Scotland).

Using the observation cycle in Chapter 2 as shown for George and Ellis' actions (Figs. 6.5, 6.6):

We can determine the following:

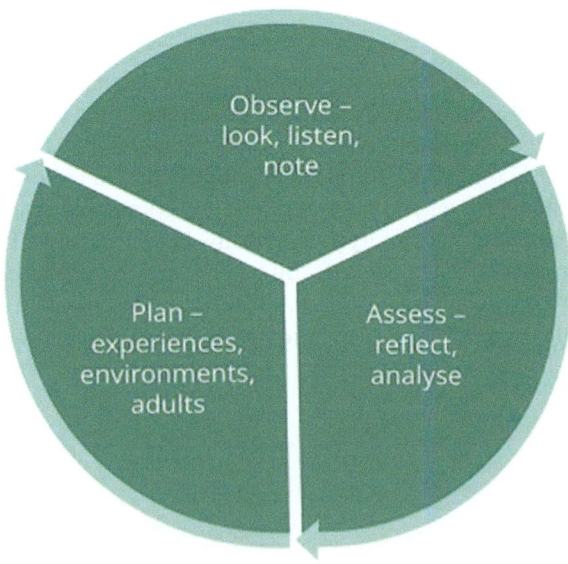

Fig. 6.5 The observation cycle (WG, 2023a)

Other Curricula Links: Realising the Ambition-Being Me in Scotland

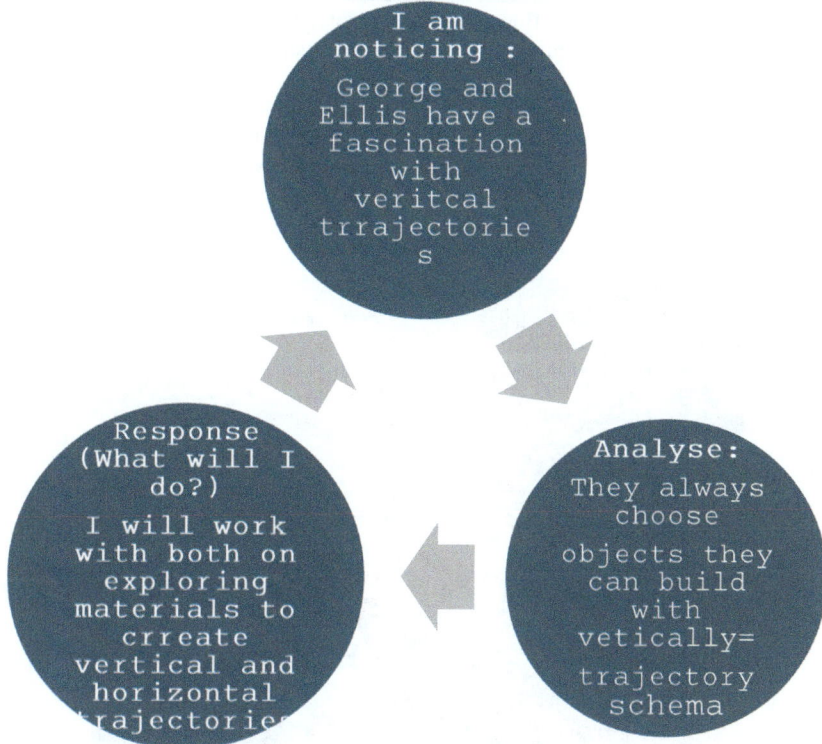

Fig. 6.6 Using the observation cycle for George and Ellis

Case Study: Harri is in the reception class at his local primary school and is 5 years old and is an only child. The practitioners report that Harri is very much a solitary child who does not really interact with the other children. He enjoys playing on his own and often speaks aloud to himself. It has been very difficult to engage Harri in any focused tasks, and he often wonders away from the practitioners, preferring to be on his own. However, the practitioners have noticed that Harri has a growing fascination with exploring vertical and horizontal trajectories.

At the water feature outside Harri is concentrating on holding a measuring cylinder steady while another boy pours water into it. He does this until the cylinder is full. Harri then carefully carries the full cylinder over to the water feature where he pours water into the yellow tubing. He watches until the water comes out from the bottom of the tubing onto the yard. Another boy comes over and asks Harri what he is doing. Harri explains, *"The water goes in the top of the yellow bit and then it runs down here and comes out here",* he points to the bottom of the tubing and the puddle of water forming on the yard below the tube. The boy goes and fetches a small silver bowl full of water and pours water into the top of the tube, but it spills over onto the boy's shoes. Both boys laugh and Harri says, *"Silly water!"* The boys abandon the silver dish, and both use the cylinder instead. Both boys carry on playing with the water feature until the end of play, taking it in turns to tip water into the yellow tubing and waiting for it to come out the other end.

Harri is using his trajectory schema to get the water to flow downwards to the floor. It has afforded him an opportunity to feel comfortable to allow another child into his play space and to work with this child to explore the downward trajectory of the water (Fig. 6.7).

Fig. 6.7 Pouring water in a downward trajectory

Here Harri's trajectory schema has allowed him to make a connection to another child with similar schematic interests. Although more research is needed into whether children with similar schematic interests are more likely to play together, it makes sense that they would, and it manifests here in this case study.

Questions to Consider:

1. Using the toolkit how could you consider meeting Harri's need to use his trajectory schema in a variety of ways?
2. How could you use Harri's trajectory schema to support him to engage more with the practitioners and the children in the class?
3. Can you recall a child that presented as a solitary child like Harri? Were there/are there any schematic patterns that might be used to nurture his schema as well as encourage him to collaborate with others?

Conclusion

This chapter has defined what is meant by a trajectory schema and how it can be observed in practice. It has explored how different loose parts in both indoors and outdoors can nurture and nourish a trajectory schema. It has highlighted how attuned practitioners can provide resources and the time and space for children to explore their trajectory schemas. This includes how features of the environment, such as pathways, slopes, tree stumps and bridges can help to stimulate children's understanding, nurturing trajectory schemas in a whole-body experience as they explore movement with their own body moving through the different types of spaces accessible to them.

Once observed, practitioners can use the toolkit to provide a range of resources that can allow children to discover new ways of learning through their trajectory schema. For example, both George and Ellis have used the building blocks both indoors and outdoors to build vertical trajectories. Whilst both boys want to build vertical trajectories, they seem to have different end goals in sight. George wants his tower to not collapse, whilst Ellis wants to build a tower bigger than him.

Whereas Harri has played with the outdoor water station as this has allowed him to observe how the water flows in a downward trajectory. He can co-operate with another child to pour water and understand that the bowl is not a suitable vessel to get the water safely into the tubing.

All three boys are identifying with Piaget's types of cognitive patterning (1969). All are linking with both figurative aspect of perception (how can I make my tower taller and how can I use a vessel that will not spill the water before it gets into the tubing?). They are all using operative cognition as they are all using thinking linked to action.

It's useful to remember that the outdoor spaces offer options that engage the senses in a different way to time spent indoors, thus learning is often deeper as a consequence. It can open more avenues to creativity, where pathways encourage whole bodily movement and language development, and the greater space outside affords exploration of routes and 'journeys'. Opportunities for imagination are further increased and horizontal trajectories become an adventure for children and a very real part of understanding the world around them.

There have been questions to consider and a case study to reflect upon. This chapter has shown how loose parts both indoors and outdoors can afford children the opportunities to explore their trajectory schema.

Reflective Questions:

1. Having read this chapter, can you think of any children you know that have a trajectory schema?
2. Harri's trajectory schema seemed to afford him the opportunity to be able to play alongside another child—something he struggled with. Thinking of children you have worked with, can you reflect upon how supporting their schemas may provide opportunities for them to co-operate with their peers?

3. Do you have different play areas for children to access, where loose parts would support a trajectory schema? What are the areas?
4. What are the loose parts? Make a list, including any outdoor landscape features as mentioned in the chapter and consider if what you have, affords sufficient opportunity for the children to move themselves and objects vertically and horizontally i.e. develop their trajectory schemas.

Key Takeaways: A List of the Main Schematic Features of a Trajectory Schema

1. **Throwing Objects**—Enjoying the act of tossing, dropping or propelling objects to observe their movement.
2. **Kicking and Pushing**—Frequently kicking balls, pushing toys or moving objects across surfaces.
3. **Jumping and Climbing**—Engaging in activities that involve moving their body through space, such as jumping off steps or climbing furniture.
4. **Running in Straight Lines**—Preferring to run back and forth in direct paths rather than moving randomly.
5. **Pouring and Dropping Liquids**—Showing interest in pouring water, sand or other materials to see how they flow.
6. **Tracking Moving Objects**—Watching cars, balls or birds in flight with fascination.
7. **Using Tools to Move Objects**—Engaging with items like ramps, slides or toy vehicles to explore directional movement.
8. **Drawing or Mark-Making in Lines**—Preferring straight marks, zigzags or lines when drawing.
9. **Developmental Significance**—Supports motor skill development, coordination and early physics concepts like gravity, force and motion.

Opportunities for Further Reading

- McCormack H (2023) Learning through play (part two) Available via: https://send-network.co.uk/posts/schemas-learning-through-play-part-two (Accessed 19th July 2024).

References

Boulton, P., & Thomas, A. (2022b). *Schematic development and the curriculum for funded non-maintained nursery settings: Toolkit.* Available via: https://hwb.gov.wales/repository/resource/39397e24-d5e9-4b57-ad15-09f64f4ad0ec/en/overview. Accessed 23rd October 2024.

Education Scotland. (2020). *Raising the ambition–Being me.* Available via: https://education.gov.scot/media/3bjpr3wa/realisingtheambition.pdf. Accessed 1st December 2024.

Gibson, J. J. (1979). *The ecological approach to visual perception.* London: Houghton Mifflin.

Louis, S., Beswick, C., Magraw, L., Hayes, L. and Featherstone, S. (2008) *Again, Again, understanding Schemas in Young Children.* London: Black.

Mairs K and the Pen Green Team. (2013). *Young children learning through schemas.* In C. Arnold (Ed.). Routledge.

Nicolson, S., & Shipstead, S. G. (2002). *Through the looking glass.* Columbus: Merrill Prentice Hall.

Piaget, J. (1969). *The mechanisms of perception.* Routledge and Kegan Paul.

Striniste, N. (2019). *Nature play at home: Creating outdoor spaces that connect children with the natural world.* Timber Press.

Taguchi, H. L. (2011). Investigating learning, participation and becoming in early childhood practices with a relational materialist approach. *Global Studies of Childhood, 1*(1), 36–50.

Welsh Government (WG). (2023a). *Observation.* Available via: View—Hwb (gov.wales). Accessed 01 December 2023.

Wilenski, D., & Wending, C. (2013). *Ways into hinchingbrooke country park.* Cambridge Curiosity and Imagination.

Chapter 7
Enclosing and Enveloping Schemas and Loose Parts

Definition An enclosing schema can be defined as 'enclosing oneself, an object or space'.

An enveloping schema can be defined as 'enveloping or covering oneself, an object or space' (Arnold and the Pen Green Team, 2010, p. 22).

Enclosing and Enveloping Schema in Action

In these images (Fig. 7.1), Ross has used the bricks (loose parts) to make an enclosure outdoors. He carried on adding bricks and a roof until he was completely enveloped inside, where he stayed all morning. He created a small opening where he could access the outside world. Phoebe is using the blocks indoors to enclose herself. She is careful to ensure she is surrounded and enclosed inside the blocks. In all these images the adults have been attuned play partners, happy to allow the children the time and space to concentrate on their intentions.

Practitioners in the setting have stated that both children repeatedly build enclosures on numerous occasions. The practitioners have noted that Ross always leaves a gap to look out of or to connect with the outside world. He has previously said this is his 'window'. Phoebe is content to keep adding blocks until she is completely enclosed within her indoor space.

Enclosing and Enveloping Schemas and Loose Parts

Some children display a cluster of schematic behaviours or sometimes two together which appear to be intertwined. Here, children are observed demonstrating both enclosing and enveloping schemas. These patterns of behaviour are seen in Figs. 7.1.

Fig. 7.1 Ross enveloped inside his outdoor enclosure

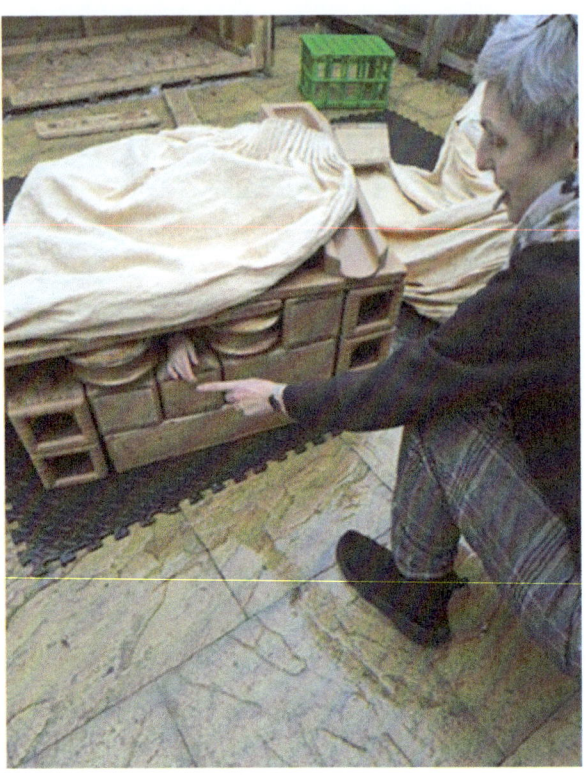

and 7.2. Practitioners had identified through observation that Ross repeatedly chooses to play with objects that can be used to cover things this includes covering himself in his play. He would build dens and often create spaces where he could place objects for 'safe keeping'. In the images, we see Ross build an enclosure and he chooses his bricks carefully, stacking them in order and choosing a specific size for his structure. He got inside his enclosure and covered himself over with the curtain enveloping himself. He remained inside the structure, covered over for almost an hour, communicating by signalling with his hand through the gap and talking. The adult did not interfere, but engaged when invited, carefully noting themes or language being used. Vocabulary was focused on terms we might associate with being enclosed and words such as 'safe', 'secret' and 'hiding'. This enveloping schema also appears in Ross' painting, and he would often paint a picture and then paint over it in one block colour, covering the painting underneath. Similarly, Phoebe has been given the time and space to enclose herself inside the blocks. She was happy to sit there and observe the rest of the children playing around her. Both these schemas can give children a sense of security or their own controllable space where they can take time out to relax and be still. Striniste (2019) talks of enclosed spaces being inviting for children to fit into and Dixon and Day (2004) propose these enclosures as being in the child's control.

Enclosing and Enveloping Schema in Action

Fig. 7.2 Phoebe enclosing herself inside the blocks

Physical resources available to children outdoors, who demonstrate enveloping and enclosing schemas are exciting and can offer much greater experimentation than those that are found inside. Wild outdoor spaces are also spaces that children believe are not owned by adults, and so children can feel more in control of their space, taking ownership, away from the constant supervision of adults (Roe, 2007). Building dens outside can be done by using branches of a tree, covered with foliage such as ferns and smaller leafy branches. Such a construction would lend itself to a collaborative task simply due to the size of the objects and manoeuvring of them into place would be easier with several small bodies working together. Senses are again heightened and often sense of smell is particularly prominent when working with natural materials, as well as texture through sense of touch. Recyclable objects such as larger wooden pallets and drainpipes can be used to create den like spaces, covered by tarpaulins or curtains, enabling enveloping and enclosing to be investigated and processed on a larger scale. These types of loose parts allow the construction to be a size that requires cognitive skills and negotiation skills as well as that which requires physical skills such as coordination, strength and balance.

Both schemas have some connection with children perhaps needing to be in control of their space and feeling safe. Moore (2015) identifies the concept of children's secret spaces which can at times be multi-faceted and is a place where children claim their domain because they are purposefully constructing their spaces away from the adult gaze (Sturm, 2008). This interest in enveloping and enclosing may be the way that Ross expresses a sense of feeling safe and secure. Enclosing ourselves in a small space can also provide a calming effect and this can sometimes allow children to self-regulate any sensory feedback, as well as any proprioception from their physical presence within the space. Being outside enables Ross to experience enhanced sensory engagement and he may have heightened sensations of being in control of his space physically as well as emotionally. Being in the outdoors may have also influenced the activity, as the space allowed Ross to build a structure that would have taken up a lot of the space indoors and his choice of materials may not have been as effective, as although there were blocks inside, they are not as large or robust so that a walled structure could be created.

Ross was inside his 'safe place' for a long time, many practitioners might have ended the activity to move onto something else, but these moments mean that often adults need to accept the child's choices and actions and withhold their instinctive responses to run their agenda, rather than let the play be the child's agenda. This is an opportunity where the adult needs to see the value in repetitive behaviours which can sometimes be labelled as a negative experience. Ross' key workers offered him valuable 'time and permission' (Clark, 2023; Grimmer & Gascoyne, 2023) and they valued his approach to investigating in this way. Time alone a place for quiet reverie and to be able to silently observe without being seen is well documented as critical for children's emotional wellbeing (White, 2008; Wilson, 1997). This aligns with Moore's (2015, p. 21) view that only children can make secret places and that adults are not capable of doing so on a child's behalf.

Enclosing and Enveloping Schemas and the Four Operating Levels

Viewing these schemas through Piaget's four levels (1962), we can see the following:

At a motor level, both Ross and Phoebe are using their actions to envelop and enclose themselves, respectively. They are assimilating which materials are needed to build a structure that will envelop them completely or enclose them. They are accommodating their actions and thoughts by choosing the correct blocks to achieve this aim. Throughout both activities, the children are assimilating the information needed to build structures of the correct size. They are reaching cognitive equilibrium once they can be completely enveloped or enclosed (Piaget 1953).

Although neither child vocalised what they were doing, Ross has on previous occasions mentioned a 'window'; this could mean that his structure is a type of *house*. This would be a symbolic representation of his enveloping schema. As introduced in Chapter 2, symbolic representation is where children use objects to represent something else. Here the gap left in the *house* Ross built has an opening which he has previously called a window. Perhaps for Phoebe being enclosed gave her a sense of being safe in a busy nursery environment. White talks of 'understanding space as a container' (2023, p. 153). Was Phoebe building herself a container where she could feel more secure? Without language, we cannot be certain. Arnold and the Pen Green team (2010) have discussed children surrounding themselves with objects as some sort of protective layer. Were the blocks Phoebe's protective layer?

Both children are using functional dependency as they are working out which blocks are a best fit to create their structures. Ross is also using an old curtain to make a roof and to keep him dry inside. He has understood that the curtain can function as a *roof* to keep him dry. It also functions as a barrier to prevent him from being seen, thus creating a secret space. He knows that keeping himself dry depends upon having a suitable covering over the top of him, but that it also provides him with a safe place where he cannot be seen.

Both are developing their thinking as they are building structures that support them in being enveloped and enclosed. They are recalling how tall and wide their structures need to be to fit around themselves. Meade has defined schemas as '…pieces of Lego which can be fitted into lots of different structures, in this instance the structures [are] cognitive structures' (Meade & Cubey, 1995, p. 2). Here both children are thinking how the blocks can fit around themselves.

Curriculum Links

In terms of curriculum links using the toolkit for the Funded Non-maintained Nursery Settings (Boulton & Thomas, 2022b) then the following can be used (Figs. 7.3, 7.4, 7.5, 7.6):

Taking the Learning Forward

For both Ross and Pheobe there are opportunities for the practitioners working with them to extend their learning, exploring materials that can be used to envelop or enclose themselves. Children love to build dens and old curtails or tablecloths can quickly become materials to make secret places to hide. Both Ross and Phoebe are engaging in problem solving of shape, space and size to craft their desired structures. They are thinking about how tall and how wide their structures need to be to accommodate them safely. This links to the exploration developmental pathway where they are exploring the properties of materials and problem solving when making dens for example (Boulton & Thomas, 2022b).

Both children are enhancing their well-being through the nurturing of their enveloping and enclosing schemas. Both children are given time and space by the adults to work on their designs. Ross has on previous occasions spent all his time outdoors enveloped within his house-like structure. The practitioners in the setting have been happy to allow him to do this without hurrying him to come out or to

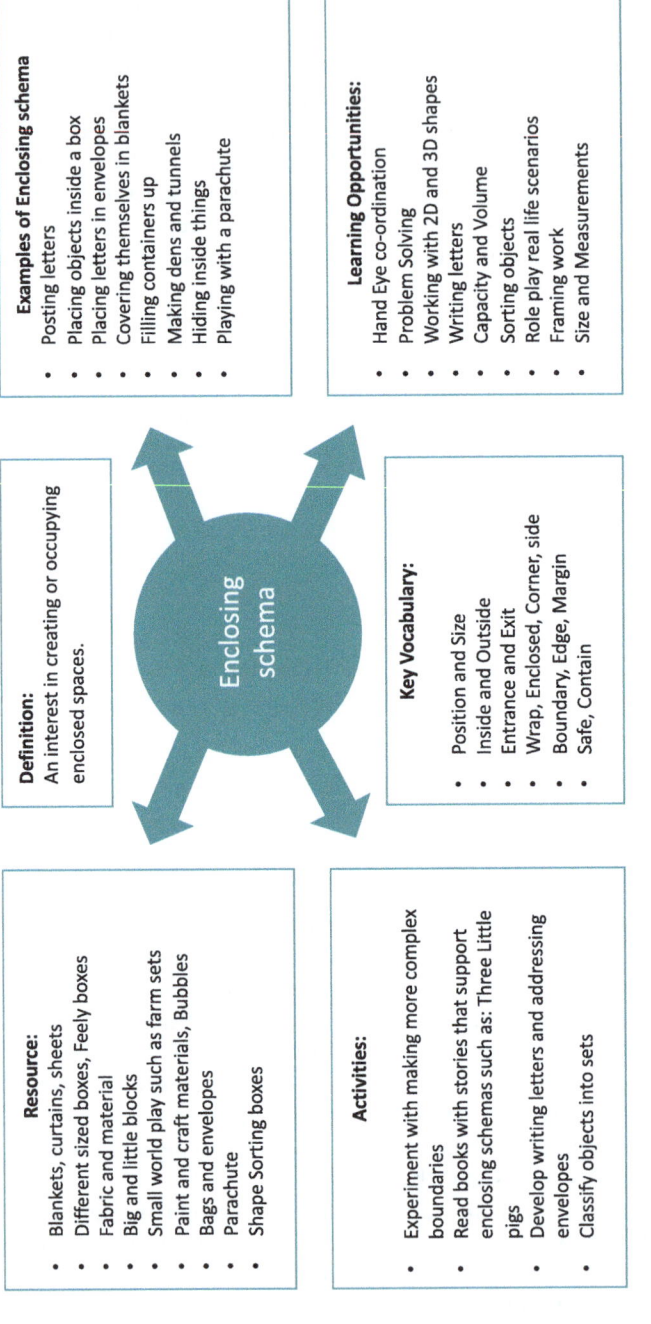

Fig. 7.3 Schemas in the curriculum: Enclosing schemas
This gives an overview of an enclosing schema and details examples of what an enclosing schema looks like in practice and planned activities, resources and vocabulary that can support an enclosing schema

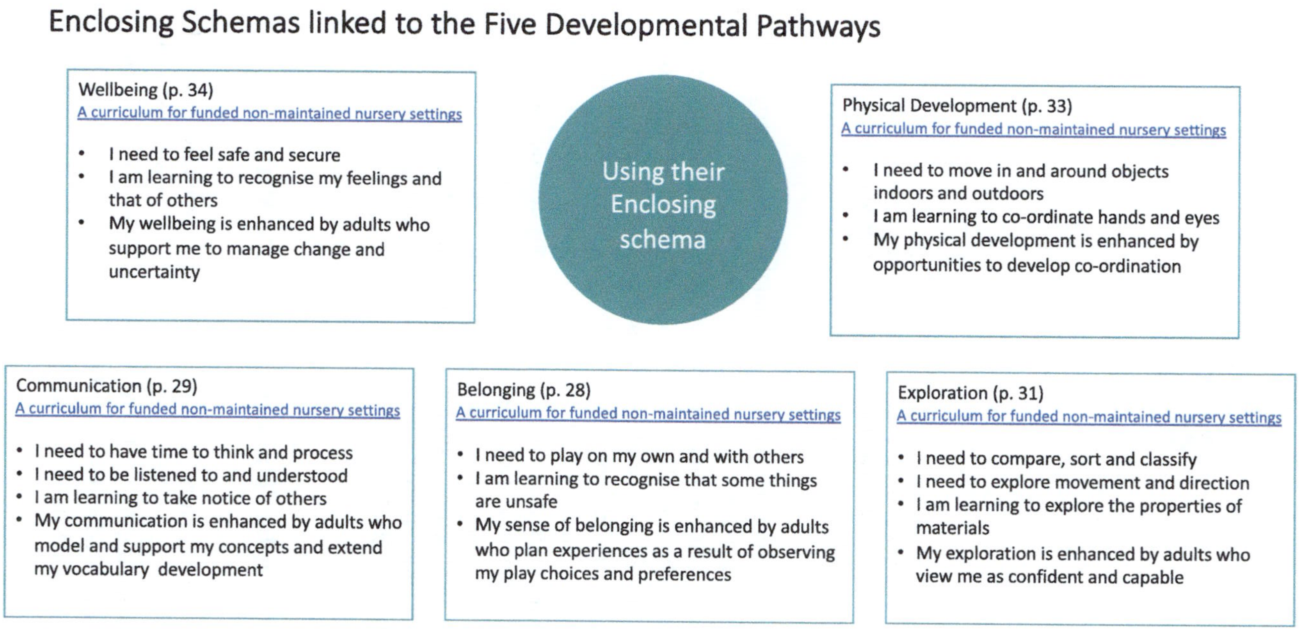

Enclosing Schemas linked to the Five Developmental Pathways

Wellbeing (p. 34)
A curriculum for funded non-maintained nursery settings

- I need to feel safe and secure
- I am learning to recognise my feelings and that of others
- My wellbeing is enhanced by adults who support me to manage change and uncertainty

Physical Development (p. 33)
A curriculum for funded non-maintained nursery settings

- I need to move in and around objects indoors and outdoors
- I am learning to co-ordinate hands and eyes
- My physical development is enhanced by opportunities to develop co-ordination

Communication (p. 29)
A curriculum for funded non-maintained nursery settings

- I need to have time to think and process
- I need to be listened to and understood
- I am learning to take notice of others
- My communication is enhanced by adults who model and support my concepts and extend my vocabulary development

Using their Enclosing schema

Belonging (p. 28)
A curriculum for funded non-maintained nursery settings

- I need to play on my own and with others
- I am learning to recognise that some things are unsafe
- My sense of belonging is enhanced by adults who plan experiences as a result of observing my play choices and preferences

Exploration (p. 31)
A curriculum for funded non-maintained nursery settings

- I need to compare, sort and classify
- I need to explore movement and direction
- I am learning to explore the properties of materials
- My exploration is enhanced by adults who view me as confident and capable

Fig. 7.4 Enclosing schema & the five developmental pathways

This shows how an enclosing schema can support a child's development through the five developmental pathways. The full toolkit can be downloaded from: https://hwb.gov.wales/repository/resource/39397e24-d5e9-4b57-ad15-09f64f4ad0ec/overview

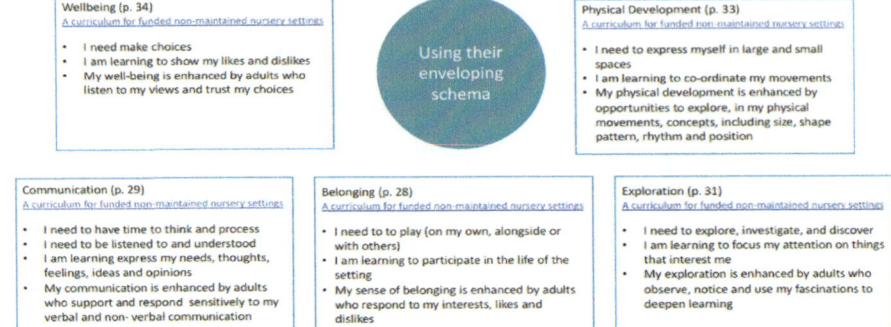

Fig. 7.5 Enveloping schema & the five developmental pathways
This shows how an enveloping schema can support a child's development through the five developmental pathways. The full toolkit can be downloaded from: https://hwb.gov.wales/repository/resource/39397e24-d5e9-4b57-ad15-09f64f4ad0ec/overview

tidy up. This means he percolates his thinking, and the slow pedagogy (Clark 2023) provides an avenue for transformative learning to take place.

In Figs. 7.1 and 7.2, Ross and Phoebe's developmental pathways are being nurtured through their play. For Ross his wellbeing is being nurtured as he is being given time to make choices, and the adults are trusting him to be completely enveloped inside his *house*. Similarly, Phoebe is also making a choice to contain and enclose herself within the bricks, an activity the adults are happy to support as she is totally engrossed in it. Both children are developing their physical development through use of hand–eye coordination. Ross and Phoebe are developing their exploration pathways as they are investigating how to build their structures successfully. The belonging developmental pathway suggests children should be given time to play on their own. Here both children are being given that time and space by attuned adults (Atherton and Nutbrown, 2013).

Other Curricula Links: The Curriculum for Wales

As discussed in Chapter 2, since 2022 Wales has introduced two curricula. One is the non-maintained for nursery settings, with its five developmental pathways and the other is the Curriculum for Wales (CfW) for learners from 3 to 16 years. The CfW aims to deliver a broad and balanced education, underpinned by four purposes and it has been developed in Wales, 'by practitioners for practitioners, bringing

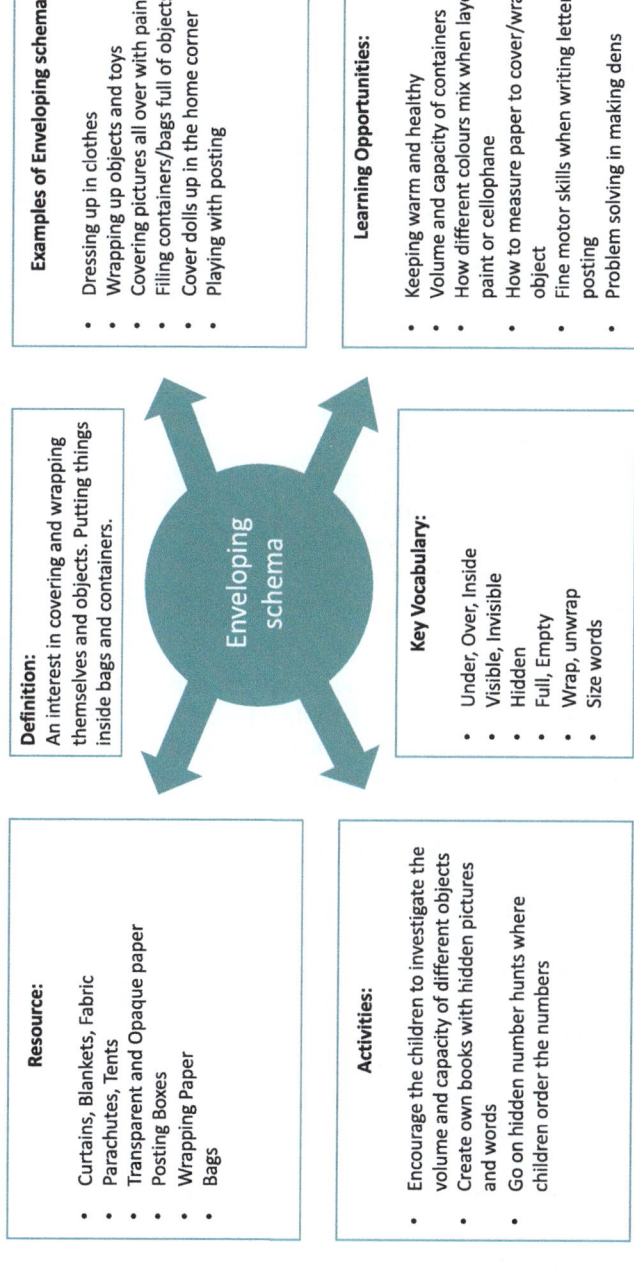

Fig. 7.6 Schemas in the curriculum: Enveloping schemas

This gives an overview of an enveloping schema and details examples of what an enveloping schema looks like in practice and planned activities, resources and vocabulary that can support an enveloping schema (Boulton & Thomas, 2022b)

together educational expertise and wider research and evidence' (WG, 2020b). The four purposes are:

- **Ambitious, capable learners**: Students are ready to learn throughout their lives
- **Enterprising, creative contributors**: Students are ready to play a full part in life and work
- **Ethical, Informed Citizens**: Students are ready to be citizens of Wales and the world
- **Healthy, confident individuals**: Students are ready to lead fulfilling lives as valued members of society (WG, 2020b)

If we consider schemas as a way that some children develop their knowledge and understanding, then nurturing and nourishing schemas will allow children to be capable learners, creative contributors and confident individuals.

Alongside these four purposes are six areas of learning and experience (AoLE's) and three cross-curricular skills which are:

- **Expressive Arts**: Includes art and music
- **Health and Wellbeing**: Includes physical education, personal and social development, and religious education
- **Humanities**: Includes history and geography
- **Languages, Literacy and Communication**: Includes Welsh
- **Mathematics and Numeracy**: Includes ICT and DT
- **Science and Technology**: Includes ICT and DT
- **Three cross-curricular skills:** literacy, numeracy and digital competence (WG, 2020b)

There are five progression steps in the curriculum from nursery to year eleven and these roughly correspond to the ages of five, eight, eleven, fourteen and sixteen.

Each of the six AoLEs has statements of what matters, principles of progression and descriptions of learning. In the mathematics and numeracy AoLE there is the statement of what matters that focuses on relationships involving shape, space and position WG, 2020b). Both the images in the photographs (Figs. 7.1 and 7.2) show both children exploring shape and size. Ross has worked out how many blocks he needs to cover himself completely, whilst Phoebe has worked out the size of the shape she needs to make to enclose herself. Progression step one states that, 'I can make estimates and comparisons with measures, such as 'shorter than', 'heavier than" (WG, 2020b). If we consider Ross and Phoebe, then they are estimating how many blocks are needed to envelop and enclose themselves, respectively. However, although schools are given autonomy to develop this curriculum, there is no mention of schemas in any of the CfW framework documents. This could mean missed opportunities for practitioners not realising some younger learners are using their schemas to construct their knowledge and understanding. Children's repeated actions could be dismissed or ignored and windows into their ways of thinking lost.

Referring back to the observation cycle as detailed in Chapter 2 (Figs. 7.7, 7.8):

If we look at Ross and Phobe's actions and use the observation cycle, then we can develop the following:

Other Curricula Links: The Curriculum for Wales   97

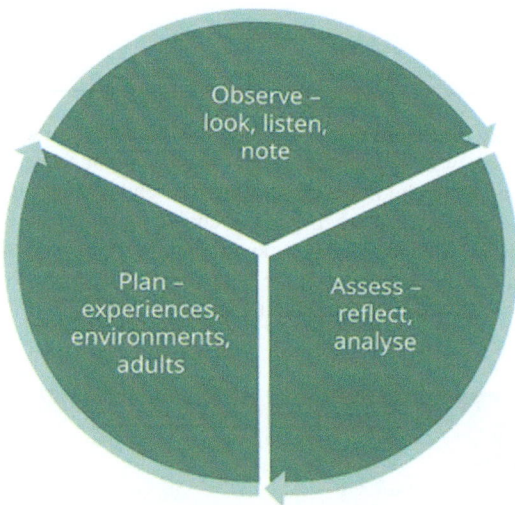

Fig. 7.7 The observation cycle (WG, 2023a)

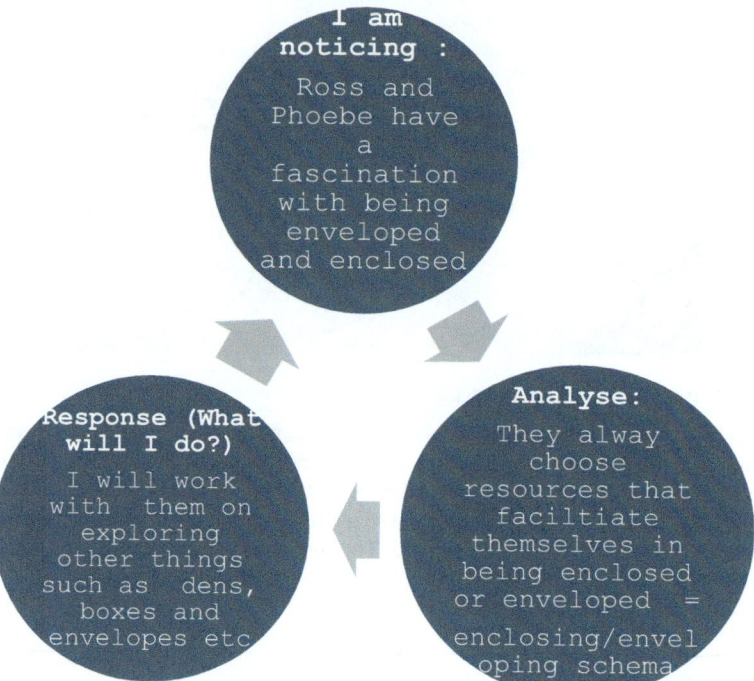

Fig. 7.8 Using the observation cycle for Ross and Phoebe

Recipe

Case Study: Today the children are outside as it is a warm summer's afternoon. The children have a variety of loose parts to play with including buckets of water and paintbrushes. One of the children, Rebecca has chosen to paint with the water. The practitioners have noticed that when given a choice of resources outside, Rebecca gravitates towards the water and today is no different. Rebecca asks one of the practitioners to chalk a rectangular shape on the ground and then proceeds to fill the shape inside with water; she stands back to admire her work (Fig. 7.9).

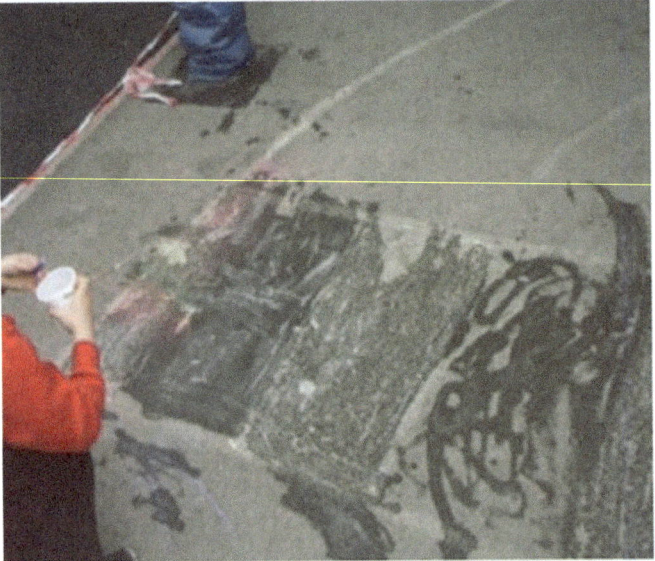

Fig. 7.9 Painting water inside a shape

As it is a warm day the water starts to evaporate, and Rebecca is quick to repeatedly repaint the 'missing' water. Rebecca asks the practitioner why the water is 'missing'. The practitioner carefully explains, in child friendly language, that the water is evaporating. They go inside to find a video to watch to explain this process. Rebecca is keen to tell everyone what she has discovered. Through being given the time and space to explore her enclosing in schema, Rebecca has been able to assimilate new knowledge and understanding about the water cycle.

Case Study: On the same afternoon Louisa is also outside, and she chooses to play with the tyres and the water. The practitioners have noticed that when given a choice of resources outside, Louisa also gravitates towards the water and today is no different. She spends a long time simply enveloping her hands inside the water within the tyre (Fig. 7.10).

Fig. 7.10 Enveloping hands inside water

She laughs as the water covers her hands and she does this repeatedly. Louisa looks around and smiles at the adult near to her. When the adult approaches Louisa was keen to show her dipping her hands in and out of the water. The adult asks what it feels like and she says, "*It's cold and it goes all over my hands-see.*" Louisa is using the outdoor learning environment to explore and investigate enveloping and enclosing schemas. According to Athey (2007, p. 47), this investigating and 'experiencing' is 'the stuff or content of the mind'. There is no pressure on Louisa from the adult not to dip her hands inside the water, or to try to direct Louisa's play into something else, instead the adult is facilitating Louisa's explorations through purposeful play by using the content available outdoors in a way that nurtures and nourishes her schema.

Here both children are using water as a loose part that affords them the opportunity to explore their enclosing and enveloping schemas. In Rebecca's case, the practitioner has facilitated Rebecca's schema by drawing a shape with boundaries which she can fill with water. The shape has enclosed her water painting. Rebecca has assimilated and accommodated new knowledge to understand why the water has disappeared (Piaget 1953).

Louisa has used her enveloping schema to cover her hands with water. Taguchi's (2011) relational materialism lens can view this play as taking place '*in-between*' Louisa and the water, where, how the water speaks to the child may also be a critical factor in meaning-making and as such transformative learning occurs between them. Thus, the affordance of the water is unique to that child and 'threads of thinking' (Nutbrown 2011) are generated, nurturing schemas. A practitioner who is not attuned to Louisa's enveloping schema could ask her to stop dipping her hands in the water but as the practitioner knows about her schema, she is happy to allow her to continue.

Louisa is having fun and as Athey states that' 'playfulness' signifies knowledge that is so well assimilated that it can be played with (1990, pp. 75–76).

Questions to Consider:

1. Using the toolkit, how could you consider meeting Ross and Phoebe's need to use their enclosing and enveloping schemas in a variety of ways?
2. What resources could you provide indoors and outdoors that will facilitate these schemas?
3. Have you enabled children time, resources and space to construct their secret spaces? What did you observe? What connections could you make with enveloping and enclosing schemas?
4. If not, then what do you think might be the barriers you experience, to affording children the opportunity to follow their agenda as they explore their schema?

Conclusion

This chapter has defined what is meant by an enclosing and enveloping schema and how it can be observed in practice. It has explored how different loose parts in both the indoors and outdoors can nurture and nourish these schemas. It has highlighted how attuned practitioners can observe children's preferred schemas and work with them to develop their knowledge and understanding. All the children in this chapter have explored both an enclosing and enveloping schema in their own unique ways. However, in each case the practitioners have ensured that the learning environment is supportive of facilitating these unique ways of discovering and learning. The activities shown have been child-led but the practitioners have been on hand to answer questions or to simply observe the play, not rushing the children or asking them to tidy anything away, slow pedagogy has been paramount in these transformative learning experiences. Piaget (1969, p. 356) stated that, 'all knowledge has to do with structures', and he identified two kinds of cognitive patterns, figurative linked to perception and operative, linked to actions. Perceptual patterns were, as considered by Athey (2007), represented through children's two and three-dimensional models as shown by drawings model making and constructions. The children are using different media to represent their threads of thinking of '*insideness*' through enclosing and enveloping. Athey (2007, p. 187) argued that 'Wherever children have plenty of material and freedom of choice in early education, schemas will be obvious to the aware observer'. Here the practitioners are the aware observers, allowing the children freedom and choice to continue to use their enveloping and enclosing schemas with different materials both inside and outside.

It's useful to remember that the outdoor spaces offer options that engage schemas in a different way to the indoors, thus learning is often different and can be more meaningful. Ross would not have been able to build his *house* indoors and Rebecca would not have been able to explore water in the way she did if she had been inside, for fear of the mess it might make and the space it would take up, as practitioners bargain the invisible constraints of a neoliberal driven pedagogy controlled by time, rather than a creative, rich, slow pedagogy driven by the child.

This chapter has shown how loose parts both indoors and outdoors can afford children the opportunities to explore their enveloping and enclosing schemas.

Reflective Questions:

1. Having read this chapter think of your own setting both inside and outside—what resources do you have that could nurture an enveloping and an enclosing schema?
2. Sometimes children will evidence their enveloping schema through painting all over their drawings—would you be supportive of this?
3. Similarly, children with an enveloping schema may want to build dens indoors as well as outdoors—how could you safely facilitate this?
4. Do you have different play areas for children to access, where loose parts would support enveloping and enclosing schemas? What are the areas and how can you develop them?

Key Takeaways: A List of the Main Schematic Features of an Enclosing and Enveloping Schema

Enclosing Schema:

1. **Drawing Circles and Borders**—Children enjoy drawing circles, enclosing objects within shapes, or surrounding items with lines.
2. **Building Enclosures**—Using blocks, sticks or other materials to create fences, walls, or containers.
3. **Grouping and Containing Objects**—Placing toys, small items or people inside defined spaces like boxes or hula hoops.
4. **Hiding or Sitting Inside Spaces**—Enjoying tents, dens or making enclosed areas with cushions and blankets.
5. **Interest in Boundaries**—Preferring activities that involve defining spaces, such as outlining shapes in sand or water play.

Enveloping Schema:

1. **Wrapping Objects or Themselves**—Covering toys, food or their own bodies with fabric, paper or other materials.
2. **Dressing in Layers**—Enjoying putting on multiple layers of clothing, gloves or hats.
3. **Filling and Covering Spaces**—Stuffing objects inside bags, boxes or containers and covering them up.
4. **Enjoying Peekaboo and Hiding Games**—Finding joy in covering and revealing objects or people.
5. **Exploring Hidden Spaces**—Crawling under blankets, inside boxes or behind furniture.

Developmental Significance

- Supports spatial awareness and understanding of containment.
- Encourages problem solving and creativity.
- Develops fine and gross motor skills.

Opportunities for Further Reading

- England L (2018) Schemas—A practical handbook. London, Bloomsbury Publishing PLC.

References

Arnold C and The Pen Green Team. (2010). *Understanding schemas and emotion*. Sage.
Atherton, F., & Nutbrown, C. (2013). *Understanding schemas and young children*. Sage.
Athey, C. (1990). *Extending thought in young children: A parent-teacher partnership*. Paul Chapman.
Athey, C. (2007). *Extending thought in young children: A parent–teacher partnership* (2nd ed.). Sage.
Boulton, P., & Thomas, A. (2022b). *Schematic development and the curriculum for funded non-maintained nursery settings: Toolkit*. Available via https://hwb.gov.wales/repository/resource/39397e24-d5e9-4b57-ad15-09f64f4ad0ec/en/overview. Accessed 23rd October 2024.
Clark, A. (2023). *Slow knowledge and the unhurried child. Time for slow pedagogies in early childhood education*. London: Routledge.
Dixon, J., & Day, S. (2004). Secret places: "You're too big to come in here!" In H. Cooper (Ed.), *Exploring time and place through play* (pp. 92–108). London: David Fulton Publishers.
Grimmer, T., & Gascoyne, S. (2023). Exploration of schema in autistic children. In C. Arnold (Ed.), *Schemas in the early years*. London: Routledge.
Meade, A., & Cubey, P. (1995). *Thinking children: Learning about schemas*. NZCER.
Moore, D. (2015). 'The teacher doesn't know what it is, but she knows where we are ': Young children's secret places in early childhood outdoor environments. *International Journal of Play, 4*(1), 20–31. https://doi.org/10.1080/21594937.2014.925292
Piaget, J. (1953). *The origins of intelligence in the child* (2nd ed.). Routledge and Kegan Paul.
Piaget, J. (1962). *Play, dreams and imitation in childhood*. London: Routledge and Kegan Paul.
Piaget, J. (1969). *The mechanisms of perception*. Routledge and Kegan Paul.
Roe, M. (2007). Feeling 'secrety': Children's views on involvement in landscape decisions. *Environmental Education Research, 13*(4), 467–485.
Striniste, N. (2019). *Nature play at home: Creating outdoor spaces that connect children with the natural world*. Timber Press.
Sturm, B. W. (2008). Imaginary 'geographies' of childhood: School library media centres as secret spaces. *Knowledge Quest, 36*(4), 47–53.
Taguchi, H. L. (2011). Investigating learning, participation and becoming in early childhood practices with a relational materialist approach. *Global Studies of Childhood, 1*(1), 36–50.
Welsh Government (WG). (2020b). *Curriculum for Wales*. Available via https://hwb.gov.wales/curriculum-for-wales/designing-your-curriculum/developing-a-vision-for-curriculum-design

References

Welsh Government (WG). (2023a). *Observation.* Available via View—Hwb (gov.wales). Accessed 20 September 2024.

White, J. (2008). *Playing and learning outdoors. Making provisions for high quality experiences in the outdoor environment.* Routledge.

White, J. (2023). Feeling at home in the world: Linking schemas with landscape and embodiment understandings. In C. Arnold (Ed.), *Schemas in the early years: Exploring beneath the surface through observation and dialogue* (pp. 137–159). Routledge.

Wilson, R. (1997). A sense of place. *Early Childhood Education Journal, 24*(3), 191–194.

Chapter 8
Transporting Schema and Loose Parts

Definition A transporting schema can be defined as 'being carried or carrying objects from one place to another' (Mairs and the Pen Green Team, 2010, p. 37).

Transporting Schema in Action

In these images (Fig. 8.1), the boys have filled up their container and are busy transporting it over to the water tray for use. Ella is busy transporting water from the trough of the easel to the bowl, and she keeps going until the trough is empty (Fig. 8.2).

In Fig. 8.3, the boys have completed their journey to the water tray. They take their time emptying out each container, placing it inside the water tray for use. This example will be further explored in the case study of this chapter.

Figure 8.4 shows Milo transporting earth in different vessels. Here he is about to tip the earth from one vessel into another. This pattern of play was being repeated as he found different vessels in the outdoor space to transport the earth from one place to another, each time repeating the same actions and taking his time to tip the soil carefully. What is interesting is that he does not position the containers near the soil that he chooses to transport, but that he takes the container to the soil, fills it up, carries it to another place in the outdoor space and then tips it out into another vessel. Part of making sense of his play is about moving himself and the earth from one place to another, and could suggest that both Milo and the soil are 'active' in this play and that they form an assemblage, where the play takes place in-between them (Taguchi 2011) and where the soil as the loose part, affords Milo the opportunity to percolate his thinking, about texture, weight, quantity and the like. He transports the materials to a place so he can make meaning through what he is doing through motion and movement. Relocating objects is a part of cognitive development and supports physical as well as psychological development. Here we also see how integral natural

Fig. 8.1 Transporting containers across the yard

Fig. 8.2 Ella transporting water from one place to another

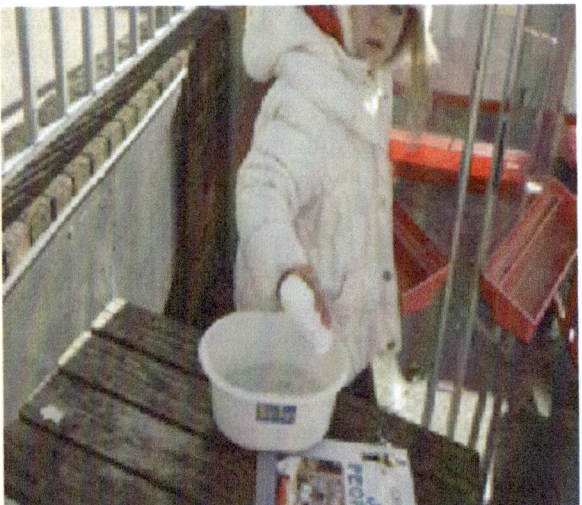

Fig. 8.3 The boys have transported their goods and are now emptying them into the water tray for use

environments are to children's development, where 'being *with* nature' instils an appreciation and value for all life and fosters a bond between child and nature itself. Milo is engrossed in play with natural materials [soil], and we observe an intense connection between the child and the soil. This perhaps also reflects White's work (2023a) on 'Ecological identity'; this is about 'being with' nature, not just in nature. Children develop a relationship with natural spaces as they do with people and the intensity of the play with the natural world is a critical element for inspiring children to learn to look after the planet. This could explain why children are so compelled to 'dig' because of the connection that is made with the soil and the earth and perhaps feeling part of nature itself (White, 2023a). Thus, nature is the responder to a child's play needs.

Transporting Schema and Loose Parts in the Outdoors

My observations over many years have identified that more than anything, that children love to move. When children are in the outdoors, there is a sense of freedom to move that affords them very different opportunities for making sense of the world. In Chapter 4 we discussed the importance of 'affordance' for children to be able to explore environments and the objects within them, each of them has values and meanings that are unique to the person perceiving them. The **'affordances'** of an object or space are all the things; it has the 'potential to do or be' (Gibson 1979). Being able to move freely in outdoor spaces affords children the chance to investigate the landscape using their bodies and brains as tools working in synergy, analysing

Fig. 8.4 Milo is transporting earth from one place to another

real experiences to make sense of what is around them, and in doing so they make sense of it in a way that is unique to them.

Transporting objects or indeed themselves from one place to another is a pattern of play that we regularly see in early years education. This is a large area of cognitive development, and it is through these actions that they start to build capacity around motion and movement, and how people and things can be positioned in one place and then relocated to another space. As in Chapter 6, the environmental landscape was seen to support trajectory schemas through lines and curves, paths and nature trails and topography of the land; and in the same way, transporting schemas can also be fed by these landscape features that seem to align with these schematic interests, helping children to meet bodily and psychological needs.

Garden paths and nature trails have an enticing draw to be followed and encourage us to transport oneself or objects along them, taking a journey along it. They are valuable in encouraging movement and enable an array of transporting activities, such as meandering along pathways, pulling wheeled toys and mobile devices e.g. wheelbarrows containing objects being taken from one point to another, and allowing the imagination to explore the spaces. Transporting schemas enable the child to physically experience mobility (White, 2023b), learning that objects can be moved in space and that they can be moved in different ways. Objects behave differently according to what they are, their size, their weight and how they travel. Children will learn that when moving objects through different kinds of spaces, where perhaps ground is uneven with bumps and holes, that they need to be handled in different ways and that these wheeled toys/objects are affected differently by gravity. Through these activities, children will be developing sensory experiences, proprioception, physical strength and coordination and learning how different objects move and feel.

In addition, as understanding concepts of movement are embedded into these activities the language that supports these schematic behaviours is also developed alongside them. Practitioners can scaffold the activities and introduce language such as 'position', 'direction', 'length', 'speed' and 'travel'. There is also the notion of how objects like a cart moves in relation to other things that exist in that environment e.g. pulling a cart over the uneven roots of a tree to transport a bucket of water. Being able to position their body or recognise that help is needed and that there is a need to work together, to generate enough power to pull the cart, builds problem-solving skills and a bodily self-awareness. Through such activities children recognise the impact that it has on the water contained in the bucket and it is what White (2023b) refers to as 'big physics', where children begin to consider what they need to do to maintain safe control of the objects being transported, as their schema is nurtured through this movement in time and space.

Transporting Schema and the Operating Levels

Viewing these schemas through Piaget's levels (1962), we can see the following:

At a motor level, all the children are using their actions to transport objects from one place to another. This resonates with White's work where she contends that children with a transporting schema have a strong interest 'in moving themselves and things/others from one place to another' (2023b, p. 145).

In the photo (Fig. 8.9b) in the case study further along in this chapter, the children have used blocks inside the wooden cart to represent seats. They are then able to sit on these seats as they are transported around the yard. Here the blocks represent seats for the children to ride the cart more comfortably. This links to what Piaget (1951) would term symbolic development. Here the children are using the blocks to represent seats. The children are consciously using one object to represent another.

The children are using functional dependency as they are working out how to transport the soil, the containers and the water from one place to another. In Figs. 8.1 and 8.3, the boys know that to get the containers elsewhere they need to place them in a truck that can be moved. They know they need to pull that truck to get it to move to the correct place. Ella knows that if she wants to move the water into another pot, she needs to tip it from one place to another. Similarly, Milo knows he needs to tip up one pot of soil into another pot to transport it.

The children are thinking about how to move the objects to get them in the right place. The boys in Figs. 8.1 and 8.3 have thought about how they can get the containers they need to the water tray.

Curriculum Links

In terms of curriculum links using the toolkit for the Funded Non-maintained Nursery Settings (Boulton & Thomas, 2022b), then the following can be used (Figs. 8.5, 8.6).

Taking the Learning Forward

For the group of boys, Ella and Milo there are opportunities for the practitioners working with them to extend their learning by providing access to a range of resources that can support transporting schemas, such as trays, crates, wheeled toys, scoops and baskets. This will enable the children to explore the different movement needed to transport materials using a range of loose parts, depending on the size of the materials or objects they want to move around. However, unless practitioners are familiar with schemas and can observe children carefully, these learning opportunities can be missed (Fig. 8.7).

Milo's developmental pathways are being nurtured through his play, and he is making choices about the loose parts he wants to use, because he is being provided with 'choice' by the adults, thus his wellbeing is considered as part of this process. His physical development is supported through agency to move around, and he is learning to move safely, developing gross and fine motor skills. In addition, practitioners are allowing him time to think and process what he is doing as he explores with different textures and 'tools', there is no rush to move him onto the next thing and the slowness of learning (Clark, 2023) means that Milo can process what he is doing in his own time, making it meaningful and authentic.

Other Curricula Links: Early Childhood Play, Learning and Care—Developmental Pathways 0–3 (Wales)

Throughout the chapters on the different schemas, links have been made to the toolkit linked to the non-maintained curriculum for learners aged 3–4 years and at the very start of the 3–16 years learning journey. However, in addition to this curriculum there is the Early childhood play, learning and care: Developmental pathways 0–3 framework (WG, 2023b). This sets out a framework for provision for children from birth to 3 years of age and uses the same five developmental pathways as in the non-maintained curriculum. For this framework, the developmental pathways are presented broadly in 12-month periods as follows:

- Here I am! (birth to 12 months)
- I'm exploring! (1–2 years)
- Look at me now! (2–3 years) (WG, 2023b, p. 3)

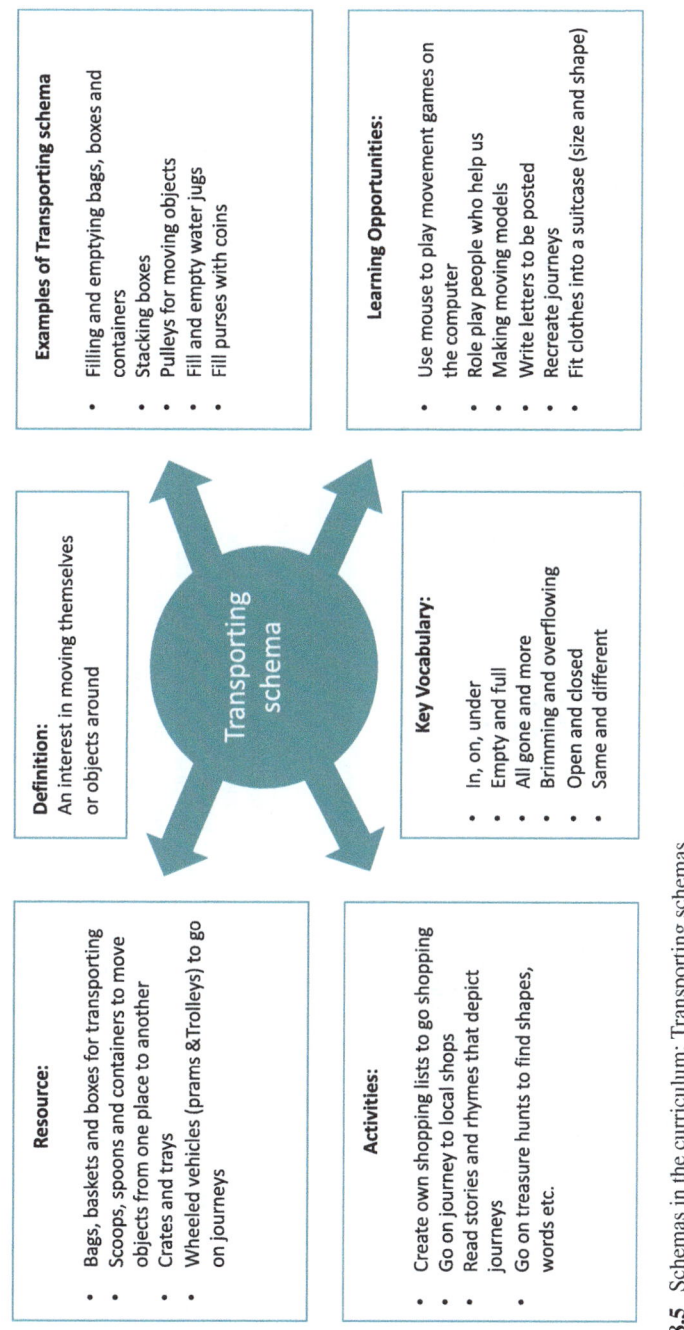

Fig. 8.5 Schemas in the curriculum: Transporting schemas

This gives an overview of a transporting schema and details examples of what a transporting schema looks like in practice with planned activities, resources and vocabulary that can support a transporting schema

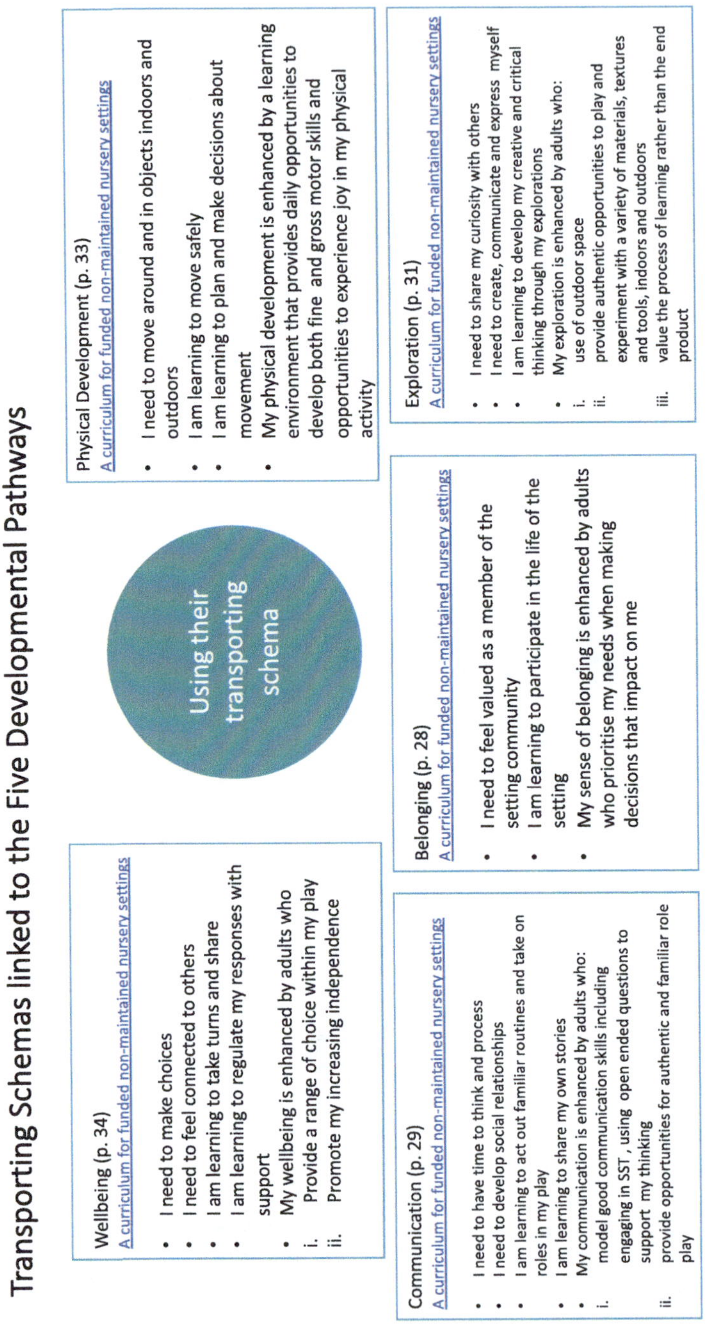

Transporting Schemas linked to the Five Developmental Pathways

Wellbeing (p. 34)
A curriculum for funded non-maintained nursery settings

- I need to make choices
- I need to feel connected to others
- I am learning to take turns and share
- I am learning to regulate my responses with support
- My wellbeing is enhanced by adults who
  i. Provide a range of choice within my play
  ii. Promote my increasing independence

Communication (p. 29)
A curriculum for funded non-maintained nursery settings

- I need to have time to think and process
- I need to develop social relationships
- I am learning to act out familiar routines and take on roles in my play
- I am learning to share my own stories
- My communication is enhanced by adults who:
  i. model good communication skills including engaging in SST, using open ended questions to support my thinking
  ii. provide opportunities for authentic and familiar role play

Physical Development (p. 33)
A curriculum for funded non-maintained nursery settings

- I need to move around and in objects indoors and outdoors
- I am learning to move safely
- I am learning to plan and make decisions about movement
- My physical development is enhanced by a learning environment that provides daily opportunities to develop both fine and gross motor skills and opportunities to experience joy in my physical activity

Exploration (p. 31)
A curriculum for funded non-maintained nursery settings

- I need to share my curiosity with others
- I need to create, communicate and express myself
- I am learning to develop my creative and critical thinking through my explorations
- My exploration is enhanced by adults who:
  i. use of outdoor space
  ii. provide authentic opportunities to play and experiment with a variety of materials, textures and tools, indoors and outdoors
  iii. value the process of learning rather than the end product

Belonging (p. 28)
A curriculum for funded non-maintained nursery settings

- I need to feel valued as a member of the setting community
- I am learning to participate in the life of the setting
- My sense of belonging is enhanced by adults who prioritise my needs when making decisions that impact on me

(Centre circle: Using their transporting schema)

Fig. 8.6 Transporting schema & the five developmental pathways
This shows how a transporting schema can support a child's development through five developmental pathways. The full toolkit can be downloaded from: https://hwb.gov.wales/repository/resource/39397e24-d5e9-4b57-ad15-09f64f4ad0ec/overview

Fig. 8.7 The observation cycle (WG, 2023a)

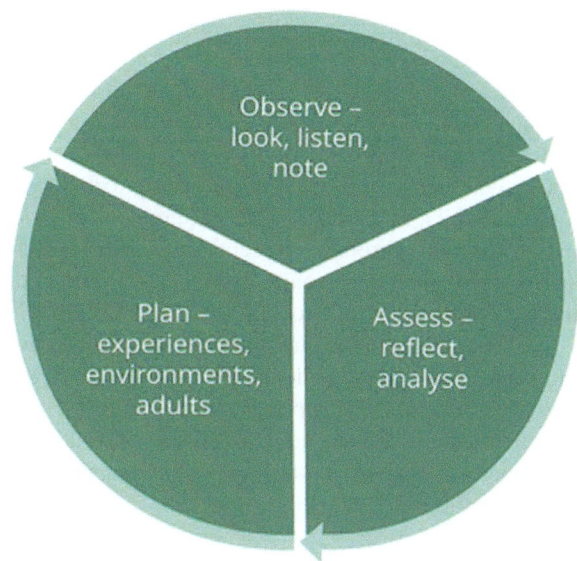

Each of the developmental pathways contains statements that begin with and expand on the following:—'I need to …', 'I am learning to …', 'My … is enhanced by …' (WG, 2023b, p. 4). The 'I need to …' statements articulate the biological and social drives that children cannot and should not ignore-these are the schemas that some children need to use to develop their knowledge and understanding. 'My … is enhanced by …' statements describe the ideal conditions that can have a positive impact on the social, emotional, cognitive and physical development of the child. Finally, the 'I am learning to …', statements demonstrate the capabilities and dispositions that children are developing (WG, 2023b).

If we look at the developmental pathways and statements for a child aged 2–3 years then, for the belonging pathway children need to be understood and responded to. In the photographs in this chapter, the children are given time to transport various objects in their own terms. This is enhanced by adults who, 'make time for me and respond genuinely to my interests, likes and dislikes' and who' create outdoor and indoor environments that provide a wide variety of play experiences' (WG, 2023b, p. 26).

For the communication pathway, adults are required to 'support me to share my ideas in my play', with children learning to 'show my thinking through play' (WG, 2023b, p. 29). In this chapter, the children are thinking about how to transport objects, soil and water from one place to another. The exploration pathway is developed through children learning to 'show my thinking through my exploration' and 'explore and experiment with purpose, both indoors and outdoors' (WG, 2023b, p. 31). Exploration is enhanced by adults who, 'notice and support my repeated patterns of schematic play' and 'understand the importance of, and give me opportunities to return to or repeat, my play '(WG, 2023b, p. 31). This framework articulates to adults the importance of observing and noticing schemas. For the physical developmental pathway, children need to learn to co-ordinate movements, and 'become spatially aware and negotiate obstacles, both indoors and outdoors'. Adults need to enhance physical development by, 'encourag*ing* me to gauge and manage risks and challenge myself' (WG, 2023b, p. 34). In terms of wellbeing, children need adults who, 'give [them] time, space and freedom to explore and discover, both indoors and outdoors' (WG, 2023b, p. 36). These elements of time, space and freedom to explore align with the theoretical concepts that have been discussed in chapters three and four predicated on the research by White (2023b) and Clark (2023), amongst others, and the philosophies of Froebel and his views on ECE (Boulton & Thomas, 2023).

If we link these to the photographs and the case study within this chapter, then the adults are allowing the children the freedom to explore and develop their cognition. However, none of this happens without careful observation with the children to note their preferred schemas. Remember the observation cycle in Chapter 2:

If we look at Milo's patterns of behaviour in the observations cycle, then we can determine the following (Fig. 8.8):

Fig. 8.8 Using the observation cycle for Milo

Case Study 1: We have seen this photograph earlier in the book (Chapter 3) where we saw how practitioners had identified Charlie's transporting schema, following some training, and through the use of some support materials which they had found, it had helped to identify this particular pattern of Charlie's play. It's worth making a revisit to this example to explore the development opportunities that ensued because of recognising Charlie's transporting schema.

Initially practitioners had not recognised this 'transporting' pattern of behaviour when Charlie was indoors, so when he was observed outside, they just thought that Charlie was fascinated with soil, but after a few weeks it became clear that Charlie was fascinated with moving objects from one place to another in the outdoors. He began to move other objects as well, including water, using jugs and a cart to do so, as can be seen in Fig. 8.1. where he is working with another child to do this.

Outside Charlie had been demonstrating a fascination of moving objects from one place to another and would fill the wheelbarrow with soil and transport it to the top of the garden area, tipping it out for the other children to use. Before returning to get more soil, he would look around for other objects that he could transport back to the bottom of the garden, e.g. gardening trowels or plastic plant pots. This was the 'job' that Charlie always wanted to do outdoors. Practitioners also noticed that Charlie was calmer and engrossed in his play in the garden area and he loved being in nature. They appreciated his passion for being in this environment and realised that a 'nature pedagogy' approach nurtured Charlie's development. The practitioners were able to view pedagogy through a different lens and understood what learning and development was taking place when Charlie was outdoors, thus avoiding 'pedagogical blindspots' (Cree & Robb, 2021). Opportunities to connect with nature need time, uninterrupted opportunities to explore and for slow knowledge (Clark, 2023) to percolate the temporal dimensions.

As depicted in Fig. 8.1 Charlie was also seen working with another child filling the jugs with water, loading them onto the cart and then transporting them to the other side of the yard to the large water tray. But it didn't end there. Once there, the jugs were carefully emptied into the top water tray and Charlie and his friend would watch the water cascade into the bottom tray and they would try to catch it in the empty jug at the bottom as it escaped through the plug. They emptied the jugs one at a time, because they had worked out that they were more likely to capture the escaping water from the bottom tray, back into the jug if they did it this way. This was important because they could then reload the jugs back onto the cart and transport the cart back across the yard. This was an activity that Charlie repeated time and again (Fig. 8.9a).

Fig. 8.9a Charlie emptying the jugs of water into the top tray and it cascades to the bottom tray

Practitioners thought that the space and freedom of movement in the natural outdoor environment had provided the agency that Charlie had needed to really explore and nurture this schema. The space gave him the opportunity to experiment, and problem solve and there was a motivation in his actions that seemed to give him purpose. Staff has noticed that through these transporting activities particularly where partner play was taking place, Charlie's language had developed and the children were heard discussing quantity and speed by deciding 'how much?' water, 'how fast?' to pour the water, so they could catch it at the bottom of the water tray, as well as 'how fast' to pull the cart, so that the water did not splash everywhere, this was indeed 'big physics' (White, 2023b). They negotiated on direction of travel and Charlie was quite specific about the position of the wheelbarrow when 'tipping up'. These sorts of opportunities afforded Charlie time to learn at his own pace (Clark 2023), to problem solve and to make decisions that were important to him, enabling him to move safely. Additionally, practitioners reported that his communication and social skills were enhanced, and his physical skills developed as he pulled, pushed, balanced and poured carefully.

Case Study 2: In Fig. 8.9b we see a slightly different example of transporting schemas as the objects being transported are the children themselves. Children with a transporting schema are often strongly drawn to moving other children in wheeled toys or carts as in the picture (Fig. 8.9b). Exploring the capacity to move people from one place to another is fascinating for children and those being 'moved' enjoy the sensation of speed and the movement itself, where all they have to do is hang on! The concept of gravity plays a large part in this action and when children have to push or pull objects that are heavy there is an inertia which acts as a stimulus to the brain, creating an internal response—which is part of proprioception. The muscles and nerves work together to transmit the messages to the brain which in turn translates them into meaning and there is a neural response, often a chemical called dopamine which makes us feel happy. This manifests in children exploring these activities for some time.

Fig. 8.9b Children transporting themselves around the yard

What followed in this group play was that the children decided they needed to be safer 'like a car', because one child banged their knee on the ground as the cart was being pulled along. So, they placed blocks inside the wooden cart to represent seats. They were then able to sit on these seats as they were transported around the yard. Here the blocks represent seats for the children to ride the cart more comfortably and this aligns with Piaget's (1959) concept of symbolic development.

Moving along in the cart, now sitting up 'in the car' and looking at where they are going further enhances the vestibular sensory system (White, 2023b) as vision and motion—detecting stimuli are co-ordinated so that balance and body control are developed. Not only are physical and proprioceptive skills being developed but these are opportunities that enhance social skills as the children negotiate that best way to move the cart, foster empathy as they consider a safer way to travel, and they symbolise

> experiences of how the world operates providing a key avenue for children to make meaning.

Questions to Consider:

1. Using the toolkit, how could you consider meeting Milo's needs to nurture his transporting schema in a variety of ways?
2. Does your outdoor space empower children to move themselves and the loose parts within it? Is it interesting? Challenging? Does it give them agency to make choices?
3. Are the children given time to process this pattern of play when they repeatedly move objects and loose parts from one place to another? What is your usual response?
4. Can you think of any children you work with that have a transporting schema? What will be your next steps to nurture this developmental process?

Conclusion

This chapter has defined what is meant by a transporting schema and how it can be observed in practice. It has explored how different loose parts can nurture and nourish this schema. Several examples have been provided which have helped to explore areas of development that are enhanced when appropriate opportunities are provided. Physical development comes to the fore as children experience movement and mobility in various ways through moving objects as well as themselves, stimulating proprioception. The sensory development that occurs through these patterns of play when outdoors also means that learning is often deeper as a consequence, particularly when time is not limited and thus the learning can be slow, percolating the neural pathways with deep, rich experiences.

The greater space outside affords exploration of moving objects through 'space and time' and problem solving can become a significant aspect of this schema as gravity and 'forces' play a part in the children moving the objects or themselves, manifesting as 'big physics' (White, 2023b) developing a range of skills and understanding. Pathways entice children to follow them moving themselves or taking their wheelbarrow on an adventure, where the play occurs in-between the child and the loose part—both players as active agents (Taguchi 2011), in ways that they consider together as they navigate the topography as well as the object being moved. An awareness of nature pedagogy by practitioners is explicit in the practices we have observed and understanding the connection between children and nature is paramount if we are to understand the opportunities that are available through the natural environment to support a child's learning and development.

Language is also developed in partner or group play through the physical act of moving objects from one space to another and then relocating them, such as 'position', 'direction', 'length', 'speed' and 'travel', concepts such as 'more than and less than', and negotiating skills are required to get to a successful result. Symbolic development has played a part in the examples with the children using blocks as seats, thus enabling themselves to now be transported safely around the yard.

This chapter has shown how loose parts, and the space afforded to children outside, particularly in natural environments, can foster opportunities for them to explore their transporting schema and as such they wallow in rich, repeated patterns of 'transporting' play, facilitating them to decipher how the world around them operates.

Reflective Questions:

1. Having read this chapter, think of your own setting both inside and outside—what resources do you have that could nurture a transporting schema?
2. What are the loose parts available? Make a list, including any outdoor landscape features and consider if what you have affords sufficient opportunity for the children to move themselves and objects from one place to another whilst exploring 'big physics'. i.e. to develop their transporting schemas.
3. Do you have different play areas for children to access, where loose parts would support a transporting schema? What are the areas?
4. Sometimes children will evidence their transporting schema by moving objects that you would prefer stayed in certain areas—would you be supportive of this? How might you manage this?
5. Similarly, children with a transporting schema may want to wheel things around indoors as well as outdoors—how could you safely facilitate this?

Key Takeaways: A List of the Main Schematic Features of a Transporting Schema

1. **Carrying Objects**—Children repeatedly move items by hand, in pockets, or in bags.
2. **Using Containers**—Baskets, buckets, boxes or toy vehicles are used to transport items.
3. **Filling and Emptying**—Continuous collection and distribution of objects from one location to another.
4. **Pushing and Pulling**—Use of wheelbarrows, wagons, or toy trucks to move things around.
5. **Collecting and Relocating**—Gathering items from one area and placing them in another systematically.
6. **Pouring and Transferring**—Moving materials like sand, water or small objects between containers.
7. **Interest in Real-life Transport**—Fascination with vehicles, shopping carts or delivery processes.

This schema helps children develop spatial awareness, motor skills and an understanding of cause and effect.

Opportunities for Further Reading

- England L (2018) Schemas—A practical handbook. London, Bloomsbury Publishing PLC.

References

Arnold C and The Pen Green Team. (2010). *Understanding schemas and emotion*. Sage.
Atherton, F., & Nutbrown, C. (2013). *Understanding schemas and young children*. Sage.
Athey, C. (2007). *Extending thought in young children: A parent–teacher partnership* (2nd ed.). Sage.
Boulton, P., & Thomas, A. (2022b). *Schematic development and the curriculum for funded non-maintained nursery settings: Toolkit*. Available via https://hwb.gov.wales/repository/resource/39397e24-d5e9-4b57-ad15-09f64f4ad0ec/en/overview. Accessed 23rd October 2024.
Boulton, P., & Thomas, A. (2023). *Schemas, outdoor play and Froebel*. Available via: https://www.froebel.org.uk/news/schemas-outdoor-play-and-froebel. Accessed January 2nd 2025.
Broadhead, P. (2004). *Early years play and learning: Developing social skills and co-operation*. Routledge Falmer.
Clark, A. (2023). *Slow knowledge and the unhurried child. Time for slow pedagogies in early childhood education*. Oxon: Routledge.
Gibson, J. J. (1979). *The ecological approach to visual perception*. Houghton Mifflin.
Cree, J., & Robb, M. (2021). *The essential guide to forest school and nature pedagogy*. Routledge.
Nutbrown, C. (2011). *Threads of thinking schemas and young children's learning* (4th ed.). SAGE.
Piaget, J. (1951). *Play, dreams and imitations in childhood*. William Heinemann.
Piaget, J. (1953). *The origins of intelligence in the child* (2nd ed.). Routledge and Kegan Paul.
Piaget, J. (1959). *The language and thought of the child*. Routledge and Kegan Paul.
Piaget, J. (1962). *Play, dreams and imitation in childhood*. Routledge and Kegan Paul.
Taguchi, H. L. (2011). Investigating learning participation and becoming in early childhood practices with a relational materialist approach. *Global Studies of Childhood, 1*(1), 36–50.
Welsh Government (WG). (2023a). *Observation*. Available via View—Hwb (gov.wales). Accessed 01 December 2023.
Welsh Government (WG). (2023b). *Early childhood play, learning and care: Developmental pathways 0 to 3*. Available via: https://hwb.gov.wales/api/storage/56774946-48aa-4fab-adda-f27508d8dc8f/early-childhood-play-learning-and-care-developmental-pathways-0-to-3.pdf. Accessed 1st December 2024.
White, J. (2023a). *Ecological identity and childhood outdoor play*. The Outdoor Teacher podcasts *[Podcast]*. September 25th 2023. Available via: The Wild Minds Podcast | Professor Jan White (theoutdoorteacher.com). Accessed: 26th September 2023.
White, J. (2023b). Feeling at home in the world: Linking schemas with landscape and embodiment understandings. In C. Arnold (Ed.), *Schemas in the early years exploring beneath the surface through observation and dialogue*. Routledge.

Chapter 9
Orientation and Positioning Schema and Loose Parts

Definition An orientation schema can be defined as 'an interest in seeing things from different angles' (Louis et al., 2008, p. 68).

A positioning schema can be defined as 'children position themselves and objects in different ways …Some objects can be placed in vertical, horizontal or oblique positions' (Arnold et al., 2010, p. 22).

Orientation and Positioning Schema in Action

In these images, David is exploring his world from different angles by orientating his body position in different ways (Figs. 9.1, 9.2). He was not supposed to hang upside down or climb on top of the blocks and he was frequently told not to do this. David was laughing as he hung from the rope bridge, and he was telling his friend who was watching him that he was being a 'monkey'.

Both rope bridge and blocks are not strictly loose part as they are fixed. But both these resources in the outdoors have facilitated David's schemas. Piaget (1953) supported the view that a child's schema is continually altered based on the activities they engage in. David had tried to climb on top of the rope bridge, but was reprimanded, so when he next uses the rope bridge, he hangs inside it instead. It could be argued that David has assimilated the information that climbing on top is not allowed and accommodated his thinking to climb and hang inside the rope, believing this will be allowed. In this way he was still able to use his positioning and orientating schema but in a more acceptable format. The setting has reported that David always tries to climb on top of the plastic cubes and then edges himself out onto the green pipe, where he stands as if he is balancing on a tight rope. They reported that on previous occasions when they have asked David to get down, he has said that he is a tightrope walker. And he has told the setting that he went to the circus recently. Although

Fig. 9.1 David hangs upside down from the rope bridge

Fig. 9.2 On top of the pipe to be a 'tightrope' walker

David did not speak whilst on the pipe this time, he was really concentrating and edged his way across, indeed like a tight rope walker.

    The practitioners are concerned over the way David is using his orientation and positioning schema. They were trying to think of alternate ways where David could safely express his schemas. One way was to consider using a range of apparatus in Physical Education lessons where David could be taught to safely climb and position his body. Athey (1990) cited in Bruce (2011) states that you do not have to love a schema, but adults need to think of more suitable ways to support schemas.

Otherwise, adults will not become 'attuned' to children's needs and ways of learning (Atherton 2014). Here the adults are trying to become attuned to David's needs by considering other ways to support his schema.

Orientation and Positioning Schemas and Loose Parts in the Outdoors

Many practitioners will be familiar with observing children using loose parts for climbing, standing on, crawling underneath and hanging from and with that comes a range of language that supports their physical actions as they engage with the objects. Often, they are used in ways for which they were not constructed, thus children's interpretation of what the objects are used for will be unique to them. The sorts of loose parts that lend themselves to orientation schemas can be blocks, logs, rope structures, sturdy boxes and tyres. Climbing frames also play a part in this behaviour (see Fig. 9.1), but this would be recognised as a fixed part. Some of these loose parts can also be observed as part of a positioning schema, e.g. crates/ boxes, blocks and smaller items such as pebbles, small world toys or any object that children develop a fascination for. In the outdoors, the space affords children to use much larger objects and often they work together to position them or indeed themselves, which sometimes means children orientate themselves in different positions using the crates, or blocks because they are fascinated by seeing things from different perspectives.

Orientation and Positioning Schemas and the Four Operating Levels

Viewing these schemas through Piaget's four levels (1962), we can see the following:

At a motor level David is climbing on top of apparatus (rope bridge and tube) and hanging inside, to allow himself a different viewpoint. Nutbrown (2011) and Nutbrown and Atherton (2013) argue that motor actions such as the above form the foundations for cognitive development, linking actions to thoughts. The coordination and connection of David's positioning and orientation schemas could result in him developing an understanding of how things look differently depending on the angle of interpretation. Nutbrown (2011) states that children can incorporate and coordinate several schemas during their development. Here it could be argued that David is combining the physical actions of positioning his body on top of objects to orientate a different viewpoint.

In terms of functional dependency and symbolic development, David has realised in that to be that 'monkey' he needs to swing upside down on the rope bridge. The action of orientating his body into a hanging position allows him to get the momentum to swing. England talks about exploring an orientation schema and positioning schema as needing a 'fair amount of risky play' (2018, p. 93). In Chapter 4, risky play was briefly discussed and David's case study is an ideal example of why it is important for the ECE adult to have knowledge of the ingredients of risky play and how they can utilise it to benefit the development of schemas. Sandseter's work (2007) highlights that children are drawn to activities such as climbing, jumping from heights, sliding fast and balancing precariously. These experiences allow children to explore the limits of their abilities and to learn to assess and manage the risks involved (Christensen & Mikkelsen, 2008).

If David is acting out a scenario of a monkey and a tightrope walker whilst hanging upside down and balancing on the pipe, then this is an example of 'thought' where David is recalling and representing an event without the need for a concrete reminder (Athey 2013). Athey states that 'playfulness' signifies knowledge that is so well assimilated that it can be played with (1990, pp. 5–76). David was laughing whilst playing at being a 'monkey' perhaps secure in the knowledge that it allowed him to combine his positioning and orientation schemas in a fun way.

Curriculum Links

In terms of curriculum links, the following ideas can be used to support planning and ideas for supporting Orientation schemas and Positioning schemas with young children (Figs. 9.3, 9.4, 9.5, 9.6):

In terms of curriculum links, the following ideas can be used to support planning and ideas for supporting positioning schemas with young children:

Taking the Learning Forward

For David, there are opportunities for the practitioners working with him to extend his positioning schema by exploring loose parts such as buttons, beads and blocks. In terms of his orientation schema David can be supported through cardboard boxes, tubes and ramps. The practitioners are not keen on how David is currently using his schemas, but they can support David in using his schema in other ways. They can set up resources in the outdoors that will allow David to explore risky play; this will facilitate David in learning to manage risk (England, 2018). David will be learning about coordination, balance, gross motor skills and problem solving.

In terms of the developmental pathways as evidenced in Figs. 9.4 and 9.6, the practitioners have tried to facilitate David's wellbeing by allowing him to follow his own interests. Albeit they have needed to find alternatives to hanging from rope bridges or balancing on pipes, but they have done this. David is developing his physical skills and his exploration skills by using his gross muscle groups to hang and balance. He is exploring different viewpoints and his spatial awareness. David

Taking the Learning Forward

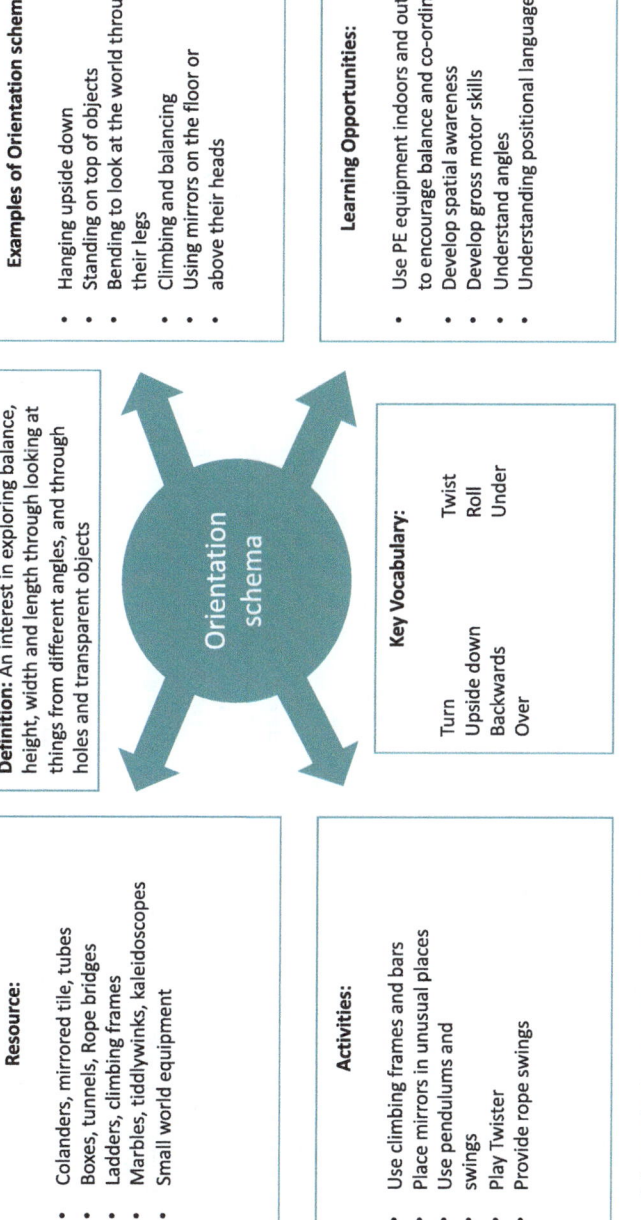

Fig. 9.3 Schemas in the curriculum: Orientation schemas

This gives an overview of an orientation schema and details examples of what an orientation schema looks like in practice and planned activities, resources and vocabulary that can support an orientation schema

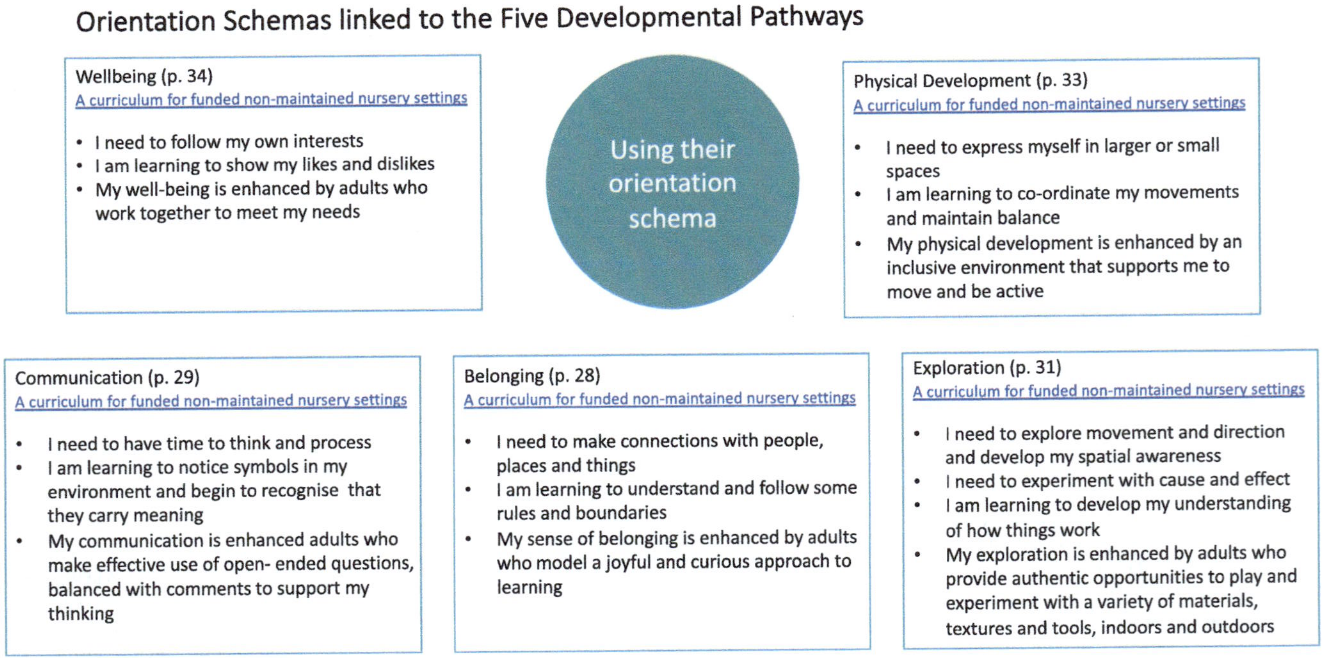

Orientation Schemas linked to the Five Developmental Pathways

Wellbeing (p. 34)
A curriculum for funded non-maintained nursery settings
- I need to follow my own interests
- I am learning to show my likes and dislikes
- My well-being is enhanced by adults who work together to meet my needs

Physical Development (p. 33)
A curriculum for funded non-maintained nursery settings
- I need to express myself in larger or small spaces
- I am learning to co-ordinate my movements and maintain balance
- My physical development is enhanced by an inclusive environment that supports me to move and be active

Communication (p. 29)
A curriculum for funded non-maintained nursery settings
- I need to have time to think and process
- I am learning to notice symbols in my environment and begin to recognise that they carry meaning
- My communication is enhanced adults who make effective use of open-ended questions, balanced with comments to support my thinking

Using their orientation schema

Belonging (p. 28)
A curriculum for funded non-maintained nursery settings
- I need to make connections with people, places and things
- I am learning to understand and follow some rules and boundaries
- My sense of belonging is enhanced by adults who model a joyful and curious approach to learning

Exploration (p. 31)
A curriculum for funded non-maintained nursery settings
- I need to explore movement and direction and develop my spatial awareness
- I need to experiment with cause and effect
- I am learning to develop my understanding of how things work
- My exploration is enhanced by adults who provide authentic opportunities to play and experiment with a variety of materials, textures and tools, indoors and outdoors

Fig. 9.4 Orientation schema & the five developmental pathways
This shows how an orientation schema can support a child's development through the five developmental pathways. The full toolkit can be downloaded from: https://hwb.gov.wales/repository/resource/39397e24-d5e9-4b57-ad15-09f64f4ad0ec/overview

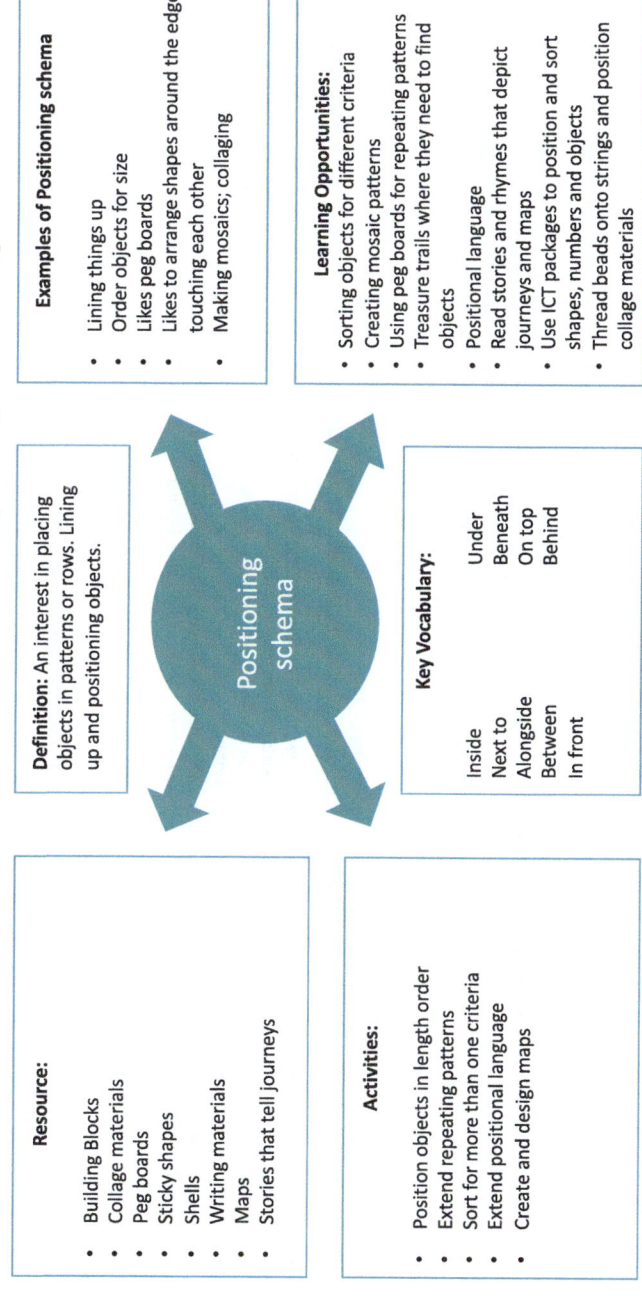

Fig. 9.5 Schemas in the curriculum: Positioning schemas
This gives an overview of a positional schema and details examples of what a positional schema looks like in practice and planned activities, resources and vocabulary that can support a positional schema

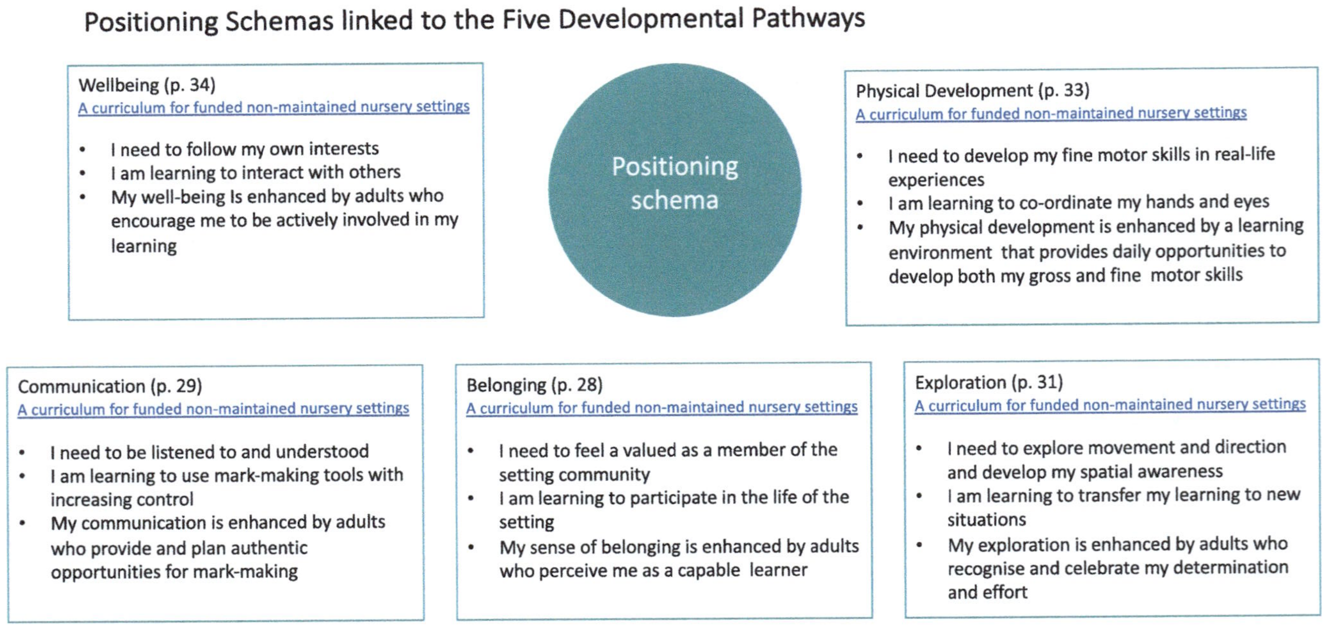

Positioning Schemas linked to the Five Developmental Pathways

Wellbeing (p. 34)
A curriculum for funded non-maintained nursery settings
- I need to follow my own interests
- I am learning to interact with others
- My well-being is enhanced by adults who encourage me to be actively involved in my learning

Communication (p. 29)
A curriculum for funded non-maintained nursery settings
- I need to be listened to and understood
- I am learning to use mark-making tools with increasing control
- My communication is enhanced by adults who provide and plan authentic opportunities for mark-making

Positioning schema

Physical Development (p. 33)
A curriculum for funded non-maintained nursery settings
- I need to develop my fine motor skills in real-life experiences
- I am learning to co-ordinate my hands and eyes
- My physical development is enhanced by a learning environment that provides daily opportunities to develop both my gross and fine motor skills

Belonging (p. 28)
A curriculum for funded non-maintained nursery settings
- I need to feel a valued as a member of the setting community
- I am learning to participate in the life of the setting
- My sense of belonging is enhanced by adults who perceive me as a capable learner

Exploration (p. 31)
A curriculum for funded non-maintained nursery settings
- I need to explore movement and direction and develop my spatial awareness
- I am learning to transfer my learning to new situations
- My exploration is enhanced by adults who recognise and celebrate my determination and effort

Fig. 9.6 Positioning schema & the five developmental pathways
This shows how a positional schema can support a child's development through the five developmental pathways

is learning to understand and follow rules, developing his sense of belonging. He has communicated his play intentions which have allowed the adults /practitioners to consider how to support David's schemas in a more suitable way.

However, unless practitioners are familiar with schemas and can observe children carefully. These learning opportunities can be missed.

Other Curricula Links-Reggio Emilia Curriculum in Italy

The Reggio Emilia approach is an innovative, child-centred educational philosophy that originated in the Italian town of Reggio Emilia after World War II. It is particularly well-regarded for its emphasis on collaboration, creativity and respect for children as active participants in their own learning (Edwards et al., 1998).

Key Principles of the Reggio Emilia Curriculum

1. **The Image of the Child**: Children are viewed as capable, competent and curious individuals with the potential to drive their own learning (Malaguzzi, 1993).
2. **The Environment as the Third Teacher**: The learning environment is carefully designed to inspire exploration, creativity and collaboration, often featuring natural light, open spaces and accessible materials (Strong-Wilson & Ellis, 2007).
3. **Documentation of Learning**: Educators carefully document children's work and thought processes through photographs, written observations and samples of their creations. This documentation informs curriculum planning and reflects children's progress (Rinaldi, 2006).
4. **Emergent Curriculum**: Learning experiences are guided by children's interests, allowing for flexibility and responsiveness to their needs (Fraser, 2012).
5. **Collaboration and Relationships**: The approach emphasises relationships between children, educators, families and the community. Learning is seen as a social process (Edwards et al., 1998)
6. **The Hundred Languages of Children**: Children are encouraged to express themselves through various mediums, such as drawing, sculpture, movement and storytelling (Malaguzzi, 1993).

Supporting Children's Schemas in the Reggio Emilia Approach

The Reggio Emilia curriculum is uniquely suited to supporting schemas because it prioritises observation and responsiveness to children's behaviours and interests. Schemas, which are repeated patterns of behaviour such as transporting, orientating, enclosing or rotating (Athey 2007) align well with the following practices in Reggio Emilia:

1. **Observation and Documentation**: Educators carefully observe and document children's behaviours, including schemas. These observations guide the creation of activities and environments that align with the children's natural ways of learning.
2. **Environment Design**: The thoughtfully designed learning spaces in Reggio Emilia often include loose parts, natural materials and open-ended resources, which invite children to engage in schema-related activities such as stacking, pouring, or constructing.
3. **Flexible and Emergent Planning**: Since the curriculum is not fixed, educators can adapt it to align with the schemas children exhibit, creating targeted opportunities for exploration, such as providing ramps for children showing trajectory schemas or containers for those exploring enclosing schemas.
4. **The Hundred Languages**: The wide variety of expressive mediums supports schemas by allowing children to explore patterns of behaviour in different contexts, such as drawing to explore rotation or constructing with blocks to understand enclosure.

By aligning learning experiences with children's innate schemas, the Reggio Emilia approach not only fosters deeper engagement but also respects and nurtures the natural ways in which children learn and make sense of the world. It fosters a relationship between the child and the environment, where the environment is recognised as the third teacher and encourages use of natural materials as Loose parts, which provides an avenue for children to learn about living things and the power of nature as a learning tool. As highlighted in Chapter 3, Nature Pedagogy is the practice of teaching alongside nature, and it focuses on nature as a valued primary factor in the learning process. The teaching and development have nature at the very heart of the experiences offered to the children, where children are noticed and their voices are heard, their interests are valued through a variety of mediums, and where the adult although aware, at times is invisible (Cree & Robb, 2021). The relationship is with 'place and space' as much as it is with people.

Viewing David's schemas through the observation cycle introduced in Chapter 2 (Fig. 9.7):

If we look at David's actions and use the observation cycle, then we can have the following (Fig. 9.8):

Supporting Children's Schemas in the Reggio Emilia Approach

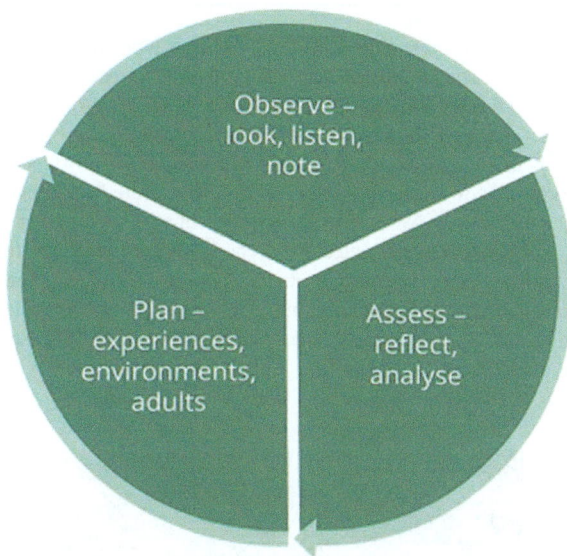

Fig. 9.7 The observation cycle (WG, 2023a)

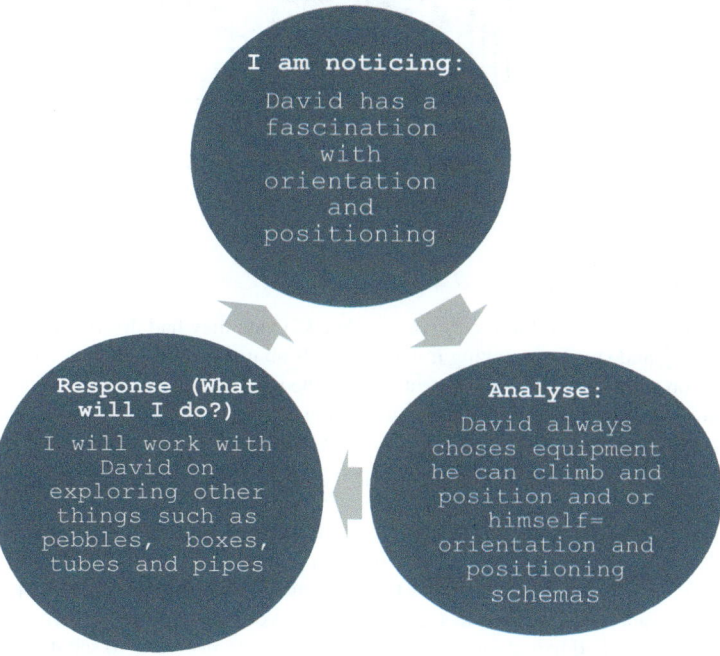

Fig. 9.8 Using the observation cycle for David (WG, 2023a)

Case Study: A group of three boys spent a long time working out how to position crates, discussing size, shape and coloured parts. Several presentations of what they did with the crates ranged from lining them up, turning them upside down and finally stacking them one on top of the other. Mathematical concepts were discussed as they considered 'width and height' as well as whilst stacking, how they would balance one on top of the other. They worked together and demonstrated negotiating skills and collaborated their ideas. Boy A was keen to experiment with positioning the crates and this aligned to the behaviours that practitioners had observed for some time, where he spent time positioning other objects in lines, e.g. blocks, or placing them in specific places on the yard where there were markings, positioning a tyre within two lines was about 'parking the car'. Language included concepts like 'first' and 'second' as well as 'underneath' and 'on top' (Fig. 9.9).

Fig. 9.9 Positioning crates

The final position of the crates was in a stack. Once they had discovered that they were strong and sturdy, by taking it in turns to climb up and stand on them, they each climbed on top giving them a different view of the yard and their surroundings. Boy B suggested they drag the crates to the fence line where they climbed up and looked out over to the adjacent field to see what was there. This corresponds with the orientation schema that Boy B manifests during his play as he repeatedly tries to climb onto or hang from objects such as climbing bars, ropes and will often climb to the top of the slide just to 'look around'. Here he orientates himself to obtain the view and perhaps considers size and distance from this new viewpoint.

Language was descriptive and they talked about the view they had from the position of the crates and what they could see because they were higher up. They spotted a ball that one of them had batted over the fence and they were now able to see it. The child proceeded to recall the game they were playing and how the ball came to be over the fence. This provided a great opportunity to recall a story, using cognitive skills where descriptions were elaborate and quite possibly not completely true, nevertheless

> it allowed imagination to develop and create a story that was keenly offered and indeed listened to and suggests that a level of deep, immersive play is taking place. This deep play manifests when time is stretched (Clark, 2023), where children are given the time to engage in their agenda, and learning percolates through the time afforded to them.

This type of creative play is supported by Froebelian theory, believing that creative play is a vehicle where 'best learning' takes place (Harding, 2024), where children become engrossed and immersed in their imaginative play. This kind of deep play evokes a deeper level of thinking and Freobel's view of how the outdoor environment promotes more freedom of movement, due to the space afforded to the children which encourages sensory exploration (Bruce, 2011), is evidenced here in this example.

Whilst this activity was being observed from afar, and adults were not part of it, it came to an end as the practitioner called the children over to resume 'learning'. It could be argued that this opportunity affords a range of learning opportunities, through this child-led interest and as such Froebel's pedagogical approach would seem to be at odds with largely mainstream teaching practice (Leigh, 2024). His principles often challenge practitioners to reflect on their practice searching for a balance between freedom and guidance and where sometimes we have to surrender the urge to control the learning, especially if observations of key patterns or learning of concepts are made, and where learning can be exploited through the children's own agenda in their play, which is their natural way of learning about the world around them.

In addition it should be noted that the 'urge to control' the learning by the practitioner seen in the case study, is perhaps created by the 'downward pressures' referred to in Clark's work (2023) created by curriculum frameworks, timetables and regimes of performativity (Ball, 2016) which were explored earlier in Chapter 3. These facets of education are perhaps what undermine the practitioner's sixth sense when observing the child who is hanging upside down and knows in their 'knower' that there is something pedagogical happening in that moment for the child but the overarching need to 'get there faster' results in the moment being 'hurried' and thus the percolation of learning is lost. A helpful prompt might be to ask 'where is this urgent place that I think I need to get to? What is it for? Whose time is being lost… the adult's or the child's? It's a challenge when the neoliberal clock is ticking, but it does require early childhood educators to have a professional confidence that empowers them to exercise their freedom and instinct, that engaging at a slower pace and stretching time (Clark 2023) is where the deep learning takes place and children's schemas can be nurtured at their pace.

Questions to Consider:

1. Using the toolkit, how could you consider meeting David's need to use his orientation and positioning schema in your setting in a variety of ways?
2. What loose parts are available to the children that might nurture an orientation and positioning schema? What can they climb on top of? Get underneath? Get inside?
3. How do you feel about the children being able to climb on top of or hang from objects?
4. What would it feel like to surrender the urge to control all 'learning' that takes place through the child's agenda to nurture your own Froebelian approach?
5. Can you think of any children you work with that have an orientation or positioning schema? What are your next steps and how can you support it?

Conclusion

This chapter has defined what is meant by an orientation and positioning schema and how it can be observed in practice. It has explored how different loose parts in both the outdoors can nurture and nourish these schemas. It has highlighted how attuned practitioners can observe children's preferred schemas and consider alternate ways to support these schemas. David has shown his positioning and orientation schemas as a constant thread of thought running through his actions (Nutbrown 2011). David has positioned and orientated his body inside the rope bridge and on top of the cube to view things from different angles and viewpoints coordinating his schemas (Nutbrown 2011). Athey (1990) suggested that children explore topological space by positioning objects including themselves. This can lead to an understanding of height, perspective, distance and spatial awareness, supporting Gardner (1984, p. 129) who argued that 'logical science and mathematics can be found in the simple actions of young children upon the physical objects in the world'.

Additionally, we have seen the three boys explore a positioning and orientation schema together. They positioned the crates, working together as well as themselves as they explored different orientations giving them different viewpoints, which enabled them to see over the fence. This opportunity, which on the surface appears to mainly require physical skills, developed into a cognitive task as mathematical concepts were discussed, as well as a range of language opportunities, which demonstrated how the boys were able to extend the initial activity from simply stacking three crates. Froebel's theory underpins this example as we see creative play as the vehicle for learning (Leigh, 2024), where children become engrossed and immersed in their imaginative play. This deep play evokes a deeper level of thinking and where the outdoor environment promotes more freedom of movement, encouraging sensory exploration (Bruce, 2011) and due to the space and time afforded to the children (Clark 2023), learning percolates through their play. However, it can be a challenge to the practitioner to step away from the urge to control the agenda and this can take confidence, practice and patience, but it is where the power and place of observation is key. This chapter has shown how loose parts in the outdoors can afford children the opportunities to explore their orientation and positioning schemas.

Reflective Questions:

1. Having read this chapter, how would you nurture David's schemas?
2. What loose parts do you have that could support an orientation and a positioning schema?
3. Can you think of how these schemas support a child's development in the curriculum you work with?
4. Would the adults you work with be supportive of these schemas? How might you support them to understand the role these schemas have in children's development?

Key Takeaways: A List of the Main Schematic Features of an Orientation and Positioning Schema

Orientation Schema (Exploring Different Perspectives)

1. **Looking from Different Angles**—Tilting the head, hanging upside down or peering through gaps.
2. **Rotating Objects**—Turning toys, books or items upside down to see them differently.
3. **Climbing and Hanging**—Seeking different viewpoints by climbing furniture, trees or playground structures.
4. **Spinning and Rolling**—Enjoying activities like twirling, rolling down hills or spinning objects.
5. **Peeking and Hiding**—Looking through holes, mirrors or playing hide-and-seek to view things from different perspectives.

Positioning Schema (Arranging and Organising Objects in Space)

1. **Lining Up Objects**—Placing toys, blocks or household items in neat rows or patterns.
2. **Stacking and Arranging**—Organising items in specific orders, such as colour, size or type.
3. **Symmetry and Order**—Displaying a preference for balance and structured layouts.
4. **Placing Things in Specific Spots**—Moving objects to precise locations repeatedly.
5. **Sorting and Categorising**—Grouping items based on characteristics like shape or colour.

This schema supports **spatial awareness, problem solving and early mathematical thinking**.

Opportunities for Further Reading

- Cree J and Robb M (2021) The Essential guide to Forest School and Nature Pedagogy. Oxon, Routledge

References

Arnold C and The Pen Green Team. (2010). *Understanding schemas and emotion*. Sage.
Atherton, F. (2014). *On repeat*. Available via https://www.nurseryworld.co.uk/content/features/learning-development-schemas-on-repeat. Accessed 24th July, 2016.
Atherton, F., & Nutbrown, C. (2013). *Understanding schemas and young children*. Sage.
Athey, C. (1990). *Extending Thought in Young Children: A Parent-Teacher Partnership*. London: Paul Chapman
Athey, C. (2007). *Extending thought in young children: A parent–teacher partnership* (2nd ed.). Sage.
Athey, C. (2013). Beginning with the theory about schemas. In C. Arnold (Ed.), *Mairs, K. and The Pen-Green-Team, Young children learning through schemas* (pp. 5–16). London: Routledge.
Ball, S. (2016). Neoliberal education? Confronting the slouching beast. *Policy Futures in Education, 14*(8), 1046–1059.
Bruce, T. (2011). *Early childhood education* (4th ed.). Hodder Education.
Christensen, P., & Mikkelsen, M. (2008). Jumping off and being careful: Children's strategies of risk management in everyday life. *Sociology of Health and Illness, 30*(1), 112–130. https://doi.org/10.1111/j.1467-9566.2007.01046.x
Clark, A. (2023). *Slow knowledge and the unhurried child: Time for slow pedagogies in early childhood education*. Routledge.
Cree, J., & Robb, M. (2021). *The essential guide to forest school and nature pedagogy*. Routledge.
Edwards, C., Gandini, L., & Forman, G. (1998). *The hundred languages of children: The Reggio Emilia approach—Advanced reflections*. London: Ablex Publishing Corporation.
England, L. (2018). *Schemas—A practical handbook*. Bloomsbury Publishing PLC.
Fraser, S. (2012). *Authentic childhood: Experiencing Reggio Emilia in the classroom*. London: Nelson Education.
Gardner, H. (1984). *Frames of mind: The theory of multiple intelligences*. London: Heinemann.
Harding, J. (2024). *The brain that loves to play: A visual guide to child development, play and brain growth*. Fulton.
Leigh, A. (2024). Froebelian approaches in primary education: A case study of topic-based learning in the primary school phase at Annan School. In T. Bruce, Y. Nishida, S. Powell, H. Wasmuth, & J. Whinnett (Eds.), *The Bloomsbury handbook to Friedrich Froebel*. London: Bloomsbury Academic.
Louis, S., Beswick, C., Magraw, L., Hayes, L. & Featherstone, S. (2008). *Again, Again, understanding Schemas in Young Children*. London: Black
Malaguzzi, L. (1993). *Your image of the child: Where teaching begins*. London: Exchange Press.
Nutbrown, C. (2011). *Threads of thinking schemas and young children's learning* (4th ed.). Sage.
Piaget, J. (1953). *The origins of intelligence in the child* (2nd ed.). Routledge and Kegan Paul.
Piaget, J. (1962). *Play, dreams and imitation in childhood*. Routledge and Kegan Paul.
Rinaldi, C. (2006). *In dialogue with Reggio Emilia: Listening, researching, and learning*. Routledge.
Sandseter, E. B. H. (2007). Categorizing Risky Play—How can we identify risk-taking in children's play. *European Early Childhood Education Research Journal, 15*(2), 237–252. Available via: https://www.researchgate.net/publication/249047571_Categorising_risky_play-How_can_we_identify_risk-taking_in_children's_play#fullTextFileContent. Accessed January 2nd 2025.

Strong-Wilson, T., & Ellis, J. (2007). Children and place: Reggio Emilia's approach to environmental education. *Children, Youth and Environments, 17*(1), 1–15.

Welsh Government (WG). (2023a). *Observation.* Available at: View—Hwb (gov.wales). Accessed 01 December 2023.

Chapter 10
The Conclusion

Recapping the Structure of the Book

This book was structured to ensure that there was a clear aim, keywords and a definition within each chapter. There were individual chapters on schemas, the outdoors and loose parts to enable the reader to have an overview of the concepts underlying the remaining chapters. This supports the uniqueness of this book where chapters five to nine explore different schemas in turn, linking to the use of loose parts, some indoors, but specifically in the outdoor environment. Each of the chapters has case studies, reflective questions and recommended reading to help link theory to practice.

The chapters on specific schemas also have links to different curricula. This allows the reader to understand the holistic nature of schemas and how they are embedded within child development and cognitive understanding. Although as authors we did not want you to think that you must link schemas to the curriculum, we were however, cognisant of the pressures of working in the early years and the need to show progress in learning which as discussed in Chapter 3 is often focused on targets, thus pedagogies that practitioners believe to be good for children are marginalised for fear of implications in a neoliberal education system. We also felt that if the only way your setting would be supportive of schemas and teaching children in the outdoors (and we have come across this) was if you could demonstrate that schemas support children's learning through showing curriculum links, then we have pre-empted this for you. Of course, it is hoped that if settings read this book, then the importance of schemas, loose parts and the outdoors will become a part of everyday pedagogy. We want the reader to have the courage to view children's actions through a schematic lens and not always through a curriculum lens. As Nutbrown (2011) so aptly stated, it is more important to focus on the processes children go through to construct their knowledge rather than measuring the end product.

Each of the schema chapters considers the essential role of observation in recognising and supporting schemas. We have included an observation cycle that can be adapted to support different schemas. It is through observation that Cathy Nutbrown's threads of thinking can be seen running through a child's actions (Nutbrown, 2011). Each of chapters five to nine gives the reader the opportunity to download a toolkit designed for supporting schemas in the early years. Although this toolkit does link to the developmental pathways seen in the curriculum for non-maintained nurseries in Wales (Boulton & Thomas, 2022b) the ideas, the supportive language and the resources to support different schemas can be used within any setting.

As chapter two makes clear, schemas are the building blocks of exploration and understanding. They represent the child's natural inclination to make sense of the world through repeated actions, be it trajectory, rotation, enveloping or connecting. These patterns are not random; they are deeply rooted in a desire to test hypotheses, explore relationships and develop cognitive frameworks that form the foundation of lifelong learning. By recognising and supporting schemas in children, educators, parents and caregivers unlock opportunities for deeper engagement. Rather than imposing rigid structures on learning, understanding schemas allows us to meet children where they are—whether that's stacking blocks to explore balance or endlessly spinning objects to understand rotation. This attentiveness fosters an environment where exploration is not only allowed but celebrated. This chapter also makes the point that not all children will show evidence of having a dominant schema. In fact, some children will not show any evidence of schemas, but for those that do, schemas are the way children make sense of their world. The following chapters consider each of the chosen schemas through Piaget's Stage Level Theory that was introduced in Chapter 2. It offers examples of the different ways young children are using their preferred schema to develop their knowledge and understanding.

Chapter 3 considers the notions of outdoor learning and play as an outdoor pedagogy and its place in supporting the development of schemas in early childhood education. It offers definitions of the outdoor approach as well as identifying the benefits of deep learning and holistic development for children's learning, by spending time in natural environments, supported by the work of Waite (2020) amongst many others. This chapter also challenges the dominant teaching approaches observed in ECE and briefly explores the varied pedagogies we see globally concerning opportunities for learning outside, recognising that for some of us there are missed opportunities for children to make real-life connections where we can make the outdoor classroom an extension of the indoors. How we perceive the term 'pedagogy' is discussed, and as part of that we have addressed some barriers to outdoor pedagogy, which include the need for training and outdoor experiences for the practitioner, upon which their own belief in this approach can be nurtured, developing the whole person, thus critically shaping the approaches used in ECE (Aoki1983 in Clark, 2023). Carlson & Clark's (2022) research plays a key role in disrupting the discourse, where slowing learning down becomes a fundamental tool in affording children time to assimilate learning at their pace and puts a spotlight on the power of outdoor pedagogies and the challenges of 'time', where we fear performativity and neoliberal thinking outweighs deep learning and enjoyment. Finally, the concept of 'Nature pedagogy' meanders its way into our thoughts and offers us the opportunity to consider how this can be a very valuable factor in our toolbox. Not only as a resource, but as a teacher, guide, and play partner, allowing nature to percolate the mind, body and soul. Our hope is that you might consider opportunities for taking children into natural environments as a central element to your practice as you seek to unearth 'pedagogical blindspots', and as you do so, that the joy of observing the *process* of learning, through connecting with nature becomes a daily habit for you and your children. Therefore, it is hoped that having read this book and specifically this chapter, it might cause you to reflect on your own beliefs and practices and that this content may percolate your own practice providing you with a firm platform to disrupt the discourse and change EC practices that will enable you to nurture 'unhurried children' (Clark 2023).

Chapter four considered the ingredients of an effective environment, exploring the dynamic relationship between the outdoor spaces, schemas and loose parts. Elements of effective environments are discussed and how they relate to creating authentic opportunities for learning and development. This includes the chance for children to create secret spaces (Moore, 2015), and it is often where we observe (undetected), schematic behaviours taking place. The theories of Loose parts (Nicholson, 1972) and Affordance (Gibson, 1979) are considered in order to provide you with a clear underpinning of why these ingredients are so critical to EC practice and a relational materialist lens (Taguchi, 2011) challenged our thinking in light of the relationship between the child and the materials, where learning and play take place *'inbetween'* them and where there are no heirarchies and each has agency and intentionality.

We have seen that Loose parts, with their open-ended possibilities and affordances, are the ideal companions to schemas. Unlike prescriptive toys, loose parts invite children to manipulate, invent, adapt and transform, giving them the freedom to apply their schemas in diverse and unexpected ways. A stick can become a bridge, a line of trajectory, or a magic wand. A collection of shells might inspire sorting, enveloping or constructing intricate patterns. 'Affordance' of an object or indeed a space is unique to each child, and unpacking this theory has hopefully helped you to view children's play through their eyes. It has provided you with some simple principles about why understanding this theory supports your planning and provision, so that you can better support the children you teach. This aspect of the chapter may also have triggered your own childhood memories, recalling how the 'sofa cushions' would make an ideal den, and it was perhaps something you found yourself repeating over and over, creating your secret spaces. Have you considered that perhaps this might have been an enclosing schema? The case study attempts to illuminate the notion of each of these theories resulting in an 'unhurried child' who is demonstrating the philosophies of Froebel, where lived experiences enable connection with nature and meaning making to take place.

Risky play was included briefly in this chapter, and although this topic could be a whole book in itself, we wanted to reference the importance of risky play and its relationship with loose parts and the natural environment, as a key ingredient in nurturing several aspects of development including that of schematic development. This chapter has considered the outdoors and the mechanics of how children engage with the world and the vital role of spaces, materials and natural surroundings in shaping that engagement. The outdoors, with its vastness, unpredictability and ever-changing resources, provides an unmatched canvas for children to express and expand their schemas.

Practical Implications for Educators and Caregivers

Each chapter has sought to give guidance on the interplay between schemas, loose parts and how the outdoors can support children's cognitive development. Chapters have provided instruction on how you as the adult can facilitate children's dynamic schemas in authentic and meaningful ways. The case studies allow adults to consider their own practice alongside answering the reflective questions. The photographs are there as a snapshot in time; to showcase the many ways children will use their schemas to develop their understanding. Schemas are a window into a child's world; ways to make what could be seen as random actions, are actually the ways that a child is finding answers and testing hypotheses.

As educators of young children, we need to be observing and adapting the learning environment to nurture and nourish their preferred ways of 'coming to know' and 'being with' the world around them. Children need time and space to explore and discover new ideas and their schemas are a key vehicle in supporting their holistic development including creativity, problem solving and imagination. The outdoors is a rich learning landscape with a diverse array of loose parts waiting to be discovered and used. Open-ended challenges can be easily posed in the outdoors that align with children's schemas. The outdoors, with its vast array of materials and experiences, reinforces the value of curiosity, allows children to embrace ambiguity, and find joy in the act of creation. By fostering these qualities in natural environments, we equip individuals to navigate the complexities of life with resilience, imagination and confidence.

What We Have Learnt as Authors from Writing This Book

For us as authors, writing this book has allowed us to shape our thinking, reignite our passion for schemas, loose parts and the outdoors and shaped our pedagogy with our students. In our role as educators of current and future practitioners we have engaged with many in-service practitioners and listened to their deep desires for wanting to provide authentic opportunities for learning and development in natural outdoor spaces, but who have been challenged by the limitations of the dominant curriculum discourse of target driven provision, which, like a thief in the night steals practitioners confidence and beliefs in what they 'know is good for children', predicated on the tensions between neoliberal performativity and real, deep, slow learning. We have been reminded of the need to recognise the importance of child-centred pedagogy and the need to teach our students the skills of careful observation in order to understand how children make sense of their worlds and to support those ways, thus bringing this into the heart of our own practice so that it is modelled to our students because 'you can't be what you can't see' (Edelman, 1960).

Schemas are not always obvious, and their patterns often emerge subtly over time. Writing this book has reminded us of the importance of slowing down, observing, and tuning into the ways children interact with their environments. At its core, writing this book has deepened our understanding of schemas, loose parts and the boundless opportunities they offer for fostering curiosity, creativity and connection. We have been reminded of the importance of play for young children and the need to be attuned playful practitioners that support the child along their learning continuum. The importance of the outdoors has been reinforced and we have re-classified in our own minds just how integral natural environments are to children's development, where 'being *with* nature' instils an appreciation and value for all life and fosters a bond between child and nature itself, and where a stick, a puddle or a pile of leaves can become a gateway to creativity and exploration. Froebel was so ahead of his time, or perhaps he was of his time, and our socio-cultural thinking and demands of a neoliberal education system have just missed the point, focusing on 'performance' and not on the 'process' of what it is to be a child. Writing this book has reminded us that the simplest materials often provide the richest opportunities, and that valuing children's natural curiosity is far more valuable than meeting targets or learning goals. In a world that increasingly values measurable outcomes and structured education, the concepts of schemas and the affordance and implementation of Loose parts and natural spaces serve as a vital reminder of the irreplaceable role of play in fostering creativity, resilience, and holistic development. Schemas, loose parts and outdoor pedagogies are not just topics we've explored—we hope they become the lenses through which you will also see the world, sparking appreciation for the complexity and potential of learning at all ages.

Pause for Thought Revisited

In the introductory chapter, we asked the following question:
What is most relevant for you to know about schemas, loose parts and outdoor learning?

We are revisiting this question now and ask you to pause and think. We hope that by reading this book you will have found it relevant and as we revisit our initial questions about schemas, loose parts and outdoor teaching and learning, it has become clear how deeply interconnected these concepts are in fostering meaningful learning experiences. We hope that you have gained a deeper knowledge and understanding of how schemas can support a child's knowledge and understanding and that loose parts afford numerous opportunities for children to nurture and nourish their schemas. We hope that you will consider outdoor spaces as a valuable resource in supporting children's schemas and that you can view natural outdoor environments as an additional 'teacher'—a primary factor in the learning process, enabling you, the practitioner, to almost become temporarily invisible to the child, and where you can learn to 'stretch-time' and gift children the opportunity to percolate the world around them into a temporal dimension. Perhaps our final reflection or challenge to you, the reader, is what Cathy Nutbrown said and what we wrote about in Chapter 2, but needs to be repeated here: 'Children's ways of learning do not change because national policies or the prescribed curriculum change' (2011, p. 128) and for some children, schemas are their ways of learning. The quote highlights an important reflection on children's learning processes, which remain consistent regardless of changes in educational policies or curricula. Cathy Nutbrown reminds us that for some children, schemas—'patterns of repeated behaviour'—are central to how they learn and make sense of the world. These natural ways of learning deserve recognition and support in any educational context.

Final Reflections…

- What elements of this book have opened a new way of seeing this aspect of children's learning and development?
- What might be the one thing that you can take away from this book and consider integrating it into your practice?
- What aspects do you think you may need to do some further reading on to foster your knowledge so that you can challenge the discourse that limits children's holistic experiences?

Remember you can access the support materials that complement this book:

> Boulton P & Thomas A (2022b) *Schematic development and the curriculum for funded non-maintained nursery settings: toolkit.* Available via: https://hwb.gov.wales/repository/resource/39397e24-d5e9-4b57-ad15-09f64f4ad0ec/en/overview
> Welsh Government (WG) (2022b) *Schematic development: noticing and supporting the repeated patterns of behaviour in children's play.* Available via: View—Hwb (gov.wales) https://hwb.gov.wales/playlists/view/1d966d4e-a1c7-4b1e-b29f-6090a3a926c7/en/1

And the reference lists will signpost you to some wonderful research that will feed your desires to be the best early childhood practitioner that you can be.

References

Boulton, P., & Thomas, A. (2022b). *Schematic development and the curriculum for funded non-maintained nursery settings: Toolkit.* Available via: https://hwb.gov.wales/repository/resource/39397e24-d5e9-4b57-ad15-09f64f4ad0ec/en/overview

Carlsen, K., & Clark, A. (2022). Potentialities of pedagogical documentation as an intertwined research process with children and teachers in slow pedagogies. *European Early Childhood Education Research Journal, 30*(2), 200–212. https://doi.org/10.1080/1350293X.2022.2046838

References

Clark, A. (2023). *Slow knowledge and the unhurried child. Time for slow pedagogies in early childhood education*. Oxon: Routledge.

Edelman, M. (1960). In Sharp, H. (2018) *Idea of the month: You can't be what you can't see*. Available at : https://ideas-alliance.org.uk/hub/2018/06/07/idea-of-the-month-you-cant-be-what-you-cant-see/. Accessed October 2024.

Gibson, J. J. (1979). *The ecological approach to visual perception*. Houghton.

Moore, D. (2015). The teacher doesn't know what it is, but she knows where we are: Young children's secret places in early childhood outdoor environments. *International Journal of Play, 4*(1), 20–31.

Nicholson, S. (1972). The theory of loose parts, an important principle for design methodology. *Studies in Design Education Craft & Technology, 4*(2). Available via: http://jil.lboro.ac.uk/ojs/index.php/SDEC/article/view/1204

Nutbrown, C. (2011). *Threads of thinking schemas and young children's learning* (4th ed.). Sage.

Taguchi, H. L. (2011). Investigating learning participation and becoming in early childhood practices with a relational materialist approach. *Global Studies of Childhood, 1*(1), 36–50.

Waite, S. (2020). Where are we going? International views on purposes, practices and barriers in school-based outdoor learning. *Education Sciences, 10*(11), 311. https://doi.org/10.3390/educsci10110311

References

Ahn, S., & Fedewa, A. L. (2011). A meta-analysis of the relationship between children's physical activity and mental health. *Journal of Pediatric Psychology, 36* (4), 385–397. https://doi.org/10/1093/jpepsy/jsq107

Alberta Family Wellness. (2013). *How brains are built: The core story of brain development.* Available on: Youtube Bing Videos. Accessed: November 2023.

Arnold C, The Pen Green Team. (2010). *Understanding schemas and emotion.* London: Sage.

Atherton, F. (2014). *On repeat.* Available via https://www.NurseryWorld.co.uk. Accessed 24th July, 2016.

Atherton, F., & Nutbrown, C. (2013). *Understanding schemas and young children.* London: Sage.

Athey, C. (1990). *Extending thought in young children: A parent–teacher partnership.* London: Paul Chapman.

Athey, C. (2007). *Extending thought in young children: A parent–teacher partnership* (2nd ed.). London: Sage.

Athey, C. (2013). Beginning with the theory about schemas. In C. Arnold (Ed.), *Mairs K and The Pen Green Team Young children learning through schemas* (pp. 5–16). London: Routledge.

Ball, S. (2016). Neoliberal education? Confronting the slouching beast. *Policy Futures in Education, 14*(8), 1046–1059.

Bennett, J. (2010). *Vibrant matter: A political ecology of things.* Duke University Press.

Bennett, N., Wood, E., & Rogers, S. (1997). *Teaching through play: Teachers' thinking and classroom practice.* Buckingham: Open University Press.

Beyer, K., Bizub, J., Szabo, A., Heller, B., Kistner, A., Shawgo, E., & Zetts, C. (2015). Development and validation of the attitudes toward outdoor play scales for children. *Journal of Social Sciences and Medicine., 133*, 253–260.

Bilton, H. (2002). *Outdoor play in the early years: Management and innovation* (2nd ed.). London: David Fulton Publishers.

Bilton, H., & Waters, J. (2016). Why take young children outside? A critical consideration of the professed aims for outdoor learning in the early years by teachers from England and wales. *Journal of Social Sciences.* https://doi.org/10.3390/socsci6010001

Boulton, P., & Thomas, A. (2022b). *Schematic development and the curriculum for funded non-maintained nursery settings: Toolkit.* Available via: https://hwb.gov.wales/repository/resource/39397e24-d5e9-4b57-ad15-09f64f4ad0ec/en/overview. Accessed 31 October 2023.

Boulton, P., & Thomas, A. (2023). *Schemas, outdoor play and Froebel.* Available via: https://www.froebel.org.uk/news/schemas-outdoor-play-and-froebel. Accessed January 2nd 2025.

Boulton, P., & Thomas, A. (2022a). How does play in the outdoors afford opportunities for schema development in young children? *International Journal of Play.* https://doi.org/10.1080/21594937.2022.2069348

Boyer, T. W. (2006). The development of risk-taking: A multi-perspective review. *Developmental Review, 26*, 291–345. https://doi.org/10.1016/j.dr.2006.05.002

Broadhead, P. (2004). *Early years play and learning: Developing social skills and co-operation*. London: Routledge Falmer.

Bruce, T. (2011). *Early childhood education* (4th ed.). London: Hodder Education.

Bruce, T. (2012). *Early childhood practice: A guide for professionals and carers*. London: Sage.

Bruce, T., Louis, S., & McCall, H. (2015). *Observing young children*. London: Sage.

Brussoni, M., Gibbons, R., Casey, G., Ishikawa, T., Sandseter, E., Bienenstock, A., Chabot, G., Fuselli, P., Herrington, S., Janssen, I., Pickett, W., Power, M., Stanger, N., Sampson, M., & Tremblay, M. S. (2015). What is the relationship between risky outdoor play and health in children? A systematic review. *International Journal of Environmental Research and Public Health, 12*, 6423–6454.

Bundy, A., Luckett, T., Tranter, P., Naughton, G., Wyver, S., Ragen, J., & Spies, G. (2009). The risk is that there is "no risk": A simple innovative intervention to increase children's activity levels. *International Journal of Early Years Education, 17*(1), 33–45. https://doi.org/10.1080/09669760802699878

Carlsen, K., & Clark, A. (2022). Potentialities of pedagogical documentation as an intertwined research process with children and teachers in slow pedagogies. *European Early Childhood Education Research Journal, 30*(2), 200–212. https://doi.org/10.1080/1350293X.2022.2046838

Carson, R. (1956). *The sense of wonder*. New York: Harper Collins.

Casey, T., & Robertson, J. (2019). *Loose parts play: A toolkit*. Inspiring Scotland. Available via: https://www.playscotland.org/resources/print/Loose-Parts-Play-Tookit-Revised.pdf?plsctml_id=10924. Accessed January 31st 2025.

Christensen, P., & Mikkelsen, M. (2008). Jumping off and being careful: Children's strategies of risk management in everyday life. *Sociology of Health and Illness, 30*(1), 112–130. https://doi.org/10.1111/j.1467-9566.2007.01046.x

Clark, A. (2023). *Slow knowledge and the unhurried child. Time for slow pedagogies in early childhood education*. Oxon: Routledge.

Clarke, S. (2006). *Mills and millipedes. Benefits of using urban settings for outdoor learning activities*. Synergy Learning. Available via: http://www.synergylearning.org. Accessed July 2023.

Cobb-Moore, C., & Miller, M. (2007). Chapter 7: Contemporary Research in Childhood Education. In J. Ailwood (Ed.). *Early childhood in Australia—Historical and comparative contexts* (pp. 94–110). Australia: Pearson Education.

Constable, K. (2013). *Planning for schematic learning in the early years*. Oxon: Routledge.

Constable, K. (2015). *The outdoor classroom in practice, ages 3–7: A month-by-month guide to forest school provision*. London: Routledge.

Cree, J., & Robb, M. (2021). *The essential guide to forest school and nature pedagogy*. Oxon: Routledge.

Department for Education (DfE). (2023). *Development matters*. Available via: https://www.gov.uk/government/publications/development-matters--2/development-matters#physical-development

Department for Education (DFE). (2024). *Early years foundation stage statutory framework for group and school-based providers*. Available via: https://www.gov.uk/government/publications/early-years-foundation-stage-framework--2. Accessed 14 October 2024.

Dixon, J., & Day, S. (2004). Secret places: "You're too big to come in here!" In H. Cooper (Ed.), *Exploring time and place through play* (pp. 92–108). London: David Fulton Publishers.

Dyment, J., & O'Connell, T. S. (2013). The impact of playground design on play choices and behaviours of pre-school children. *Children's Geographies, 11*(3), 263–280. https://doi.org/10.1080/14733285.2013.812272

Edelman, M. (1960) in Sharp, H. (2018) *Idea of the month: You can't be what you can't see*. Available at: https://ideas-alliance.org.uk/hub/2018/06/07/idea-of-the-month-you-cant-be-what-you-cant-see/. Accessed October 2024.

Education Scotland. (2020). *Realising the ambition: Being me.* Education Scotland.

Edwards, C., Gandini, L., & Forman, G. (1998). *The hundred languages of children: The Reggio Emilia approach—Advanced reflections.* Ablex Publishing Corporation.

England, L. (2018). *Schemas—A practical handbook.* London: Bloomsbury Publishing PLC.

Englen, L., Bundy, A., Naughton, G., Simpson, J. M., Bauman, A., Ragen, J., Baur, L., Wyver, S., Tranter, P.,Niehues, A., Schiller, W., Perry, G., Jessup, G., & vander Ploeg, H. P. (2013). Increasing physical activity in young primary school children in child's play: A cluster randomised controlled trial. *Preventative medicine, 56*(5), 319–325.

English Outdoor Council. (2018). *What is outdoor learning?* Available via: English Outdoor Council: What is Outdoor Learning? Accessed Sept 2023.

Forman, G. (1994). Different media, different languages. In L. G. Katz & B. Cesarone (Eds.), *Reflections on the Reggio Emilia approach* (pp. 41–54). ERIC Clearinghouse on Elementary Early Childhood Education.

Fraser, S. (2012). *Authentic childhood: Experiencing Reggio Emilia in the classroom.* London: Nelson Education.

Frost, J. (1990). The early childhood playground. *Young Children, 45*(20), 81–82.

Gardner, H. (1984). *Frames of mind: The theory of multiple intelligences.* London: Heinemann.

Gardner, H. (1999). *Intelligence reframed: Multiple intelligences for the 21st century.* New York: Basic Books.

Gaver, W. (1991). *Technology affordances.* In CHI'91. New Orleans. United States. [Conference Item]. https://doi.org/10.1145/108844.108856

Gibson, J. J. (1979). *The ecological approach to visual perception.* Mifflin: Houghton.

Gibson, J. L., Cornell, M., & Gill, T. (2017). A systematic review of research into the impact of loose parts play on children's cognitive, social and emotional development. *School Mental Health, 9,* 295–309. https://doi.org/10.1007/s12310-017-9220-9

Gill, T. (2007). *No fear: Growing up in a risk averse society.* London: Calouste Gulbenkian Foundation.

Gray, P. (2013). *Free to learn.* New York: Basic Books.

Green, D., & Clark, A. (2024). *A Froebelian approach time for childhood: A slow pedagogy.* Available via: https://www.froebel.org.uk/uploads/documents/FT_Slow-Pedagogy_pamphlet.pdf. Accessed January 2025.

Grimmer, T., & Gascoyne, S. (2023). Exploration of schema in autistic children. In C. Arnold (Ed.), *Schemas in the early years.* London: Routledge.

Halpenny, A., & Pettersen, J. (2014). *Introducing Piaget.* Oxon: Routledge.

Harding, J. (2024). *The brain that loves to play: A visual guide to child development, play and brain growth.* London: Fulton.

Hinds, J., & Sparks, P. (2008). Engaging with the natural environment: The role of affective connection and identity. *Journal of Environmental Psychology., 28,* 109–120.

Hobson, T. (2020). *Integrating loose parts play in a preschool program.* Available via: https://edutopia.org/article/integrating-loose-parts-play-preschool-program?utm_content=linkspos5&utm_campaign=weekly-202-1-18&utm_source=edu-legacy&utm_medium=email. Accessed September 2024.

Institute of Outdoor Learning. (2023). *What is outdoor learning?* Available via: https://www.outdoor-learning.org/about/about-outdoor-learning.html. Accessed September 2023.

International School of Macaco (ISM). (2018). *Outdoor play and child development.* Available at: https://tis.edu.mo/news/outdoor-play-and-child-development. Accessed October 2022.

James, D. (2012). *Survey of the impact of scrapstore playpod in primary schools.* Children's Scrapstore.

James, J. K., & Williams, T. (2017). School-based experiential outdoor education: A neglected necessity. *The Journal of Experiential Education, 40*(1), 58–71. https://doi.org/10.1177/1053825916676190

Johnson, P. (2013). Schoolyard geographies: The influence of object-play and place-making on relationships. *Review of International Geographical Education, 3*(1), 77–92.

Lavrysen, A., Bertrands, E., Leyssen, L., Smets, L., Vanderspikken, A., & De Graef, P. (2017). Risky-play at school: Facilitating risk perception and competence in young children. *European Early Childhood Education Research Journal, 25*(1), 89–105.

Learning and Teaching Scotland. (2010). *Curriculum for excellence through outdoor learning*. Available via: https://education.gov.scot/documents/cfe-through-outdoor-learning.pdf. Accessed December 2023.

Leather, M. (2018). Outdoor education in the national curriculum: The shifting sands in formal education. In P. B. Becker, C. L. Humberstone, & J. Schirp (Eds.), *The changing world of outdoor learning in Europe* (pp. 179–193). London: Routledge.

Leigh, A. (2024). Froebelian approaches in primary education: A case study of topic-based learning in the primary school phase at Annan School. In T. Bruce, Y. Nishida, S. Powell, H. Wasmuth, & J. Whinnett (Eds.), *The Bloomsbury handbook to Friedrich Froebel*. London: Bloomsbury Academic.

Lester, O., Jones, O., & Russell, W. (2010). *Supporting school improvement through play: An evaluation of South Gloucestershire's outdoor play and learning programme*. Play England.

Lilley, I. (1967). *Friedrich Froebel. A selection of writings*. Cambridge University Press.

Louis, S. (2016). *The importance of schemas in every child's learning*. Available via: https://www.communityplaythings.co.uk/learning-library/articles/schemas-by-stella-louis#:~:text=The%20revised%20EYFS%20(2012)%20acknowledges,sometimes%20referred%20to%20as%20schemas. Accessed 29 April 2024.

Louis, S., Beswick, C., Magraw, L., Hayes, L., & Featherstone, S. (2008). *Again, again, understanding schemas in young children*. London: A&C Black publishers Limited.

Louv, R. (2009). *Last child in the woods: Saving our children from nature deficit-disorder*. London: Atlantic Books.

MacQuarrie, S. (2018). Everyday teaching and outdoor learning: Developing an integrated approach to support school-based provision. *Education 3–13, 46*(3), 45–361. https://doi.org/10.1080/03004279.2016.1263968

Mairs, K., & the Pen Green Team. (2013). *Young children learning through schemas*. C. Arnold (Ed.). London, Routledge.

Malaguzzi, L. (1993). *Your image of the child: Where teaching begins*. London: Exchange Press.

Mayer, F. S., & Frantz, C. M. (2004). The connectedness to nature scale: A measure of individuals' feeling in community with nature. *Journal of Environmental Psychology, 24*, 503–515.

Maynard, T., & Thomas, N. (2009). *Early childhood studies* (2nd ed.). London: Sage.

Maynard, T., & Waters, J. (2007). Learning in the outdoor environment: A missed opportunity? *Journal of Early Years, 27*(3), 255–265.

Maynard, T., Waters, J., & Clement, J. (2013). Child-initiated learning, the outdoor environment and the 'underachieving' child. *Early Years: an International Research Journal, 33*(3), 212–225. https://doi.org/10.1080/09575146.2013.771152

McVee, M., Dunsmore, K., & Gavelek, J. (2005). Schema theory revisited. *Review of Educational Research, 75*(4), 531–566.

Meade, A., & Cubey, P. (1995). *Thinking children: Learning about schemas*. NZCER.

Meade, A., & Cubey, P. (2008). *Thinking children, learning about schemas*. Open University.

Meltzoff, A., & Moore, M. (1998). Object representation, identity, and the paradox of early permanence: Steps toward a new framework. *Infant Behaviour and Development, 21*(2), 201–235.

Moore, D. (2015). 'The teacher doesn't know what it is, but she knows where we are': Young children's secret places in early childhood outdoor environments. *International Journal of Play, 4*(1), 20–31. https://doi.org/10.1080/21594937.2014.925292

Moser, T., & Martinsen, M. T. (2010). The outdoor environment in Norwegian Kindergartens as Pedagogical Spaces for Toddlers Play, learning and development. *European Early Childhood Education Research Journal, 18*(4), 457–471.

Mygind, E., Bølling, M., & Barfod, K. S. (2019). Primary teachers' experiences with weekly education outside the classroom during a year. *Education 3–13, 47*(5), 599–611. https://doi.org/10.1080/03004279.2018.1513544

Nedovic, S., & Morrisey, A. (2013). Calm active and focused: Children's responses to an organic outdoor learning environment. *Learning Environment Research, 16*, 281–295. https://doi.org/10/1007/s10984-013-9127-9

Neisser, U. (1976). *Cognition and reality*. San Francisco: W. H. Freeman.

Nicholson, S. (1972). The theory of loose parts, an important principle for design methodology. *Studies in Design Education Craft and Technology, 4*(2). Available via: http://jil.lboro.ac.uk/ojs/index.php/SDEC/article/view/1204

Nicolson, S., & Shipstead, S. G. (2002). *Through the looking glass*. Columbus: Merrill Prentice Hall.

Nutbrown, C. (2006). *Key concepts in early childhood education and care*. London: Sage.

Nutbrown, C. (2011). *Threads of thinking schemas and young children's learning* (4th ed.). London: Sage.

Oberle, E., Zeni, M., Munday, F., & Brussoni, M. (2021). Support factors and barriers for outdoor learning in elementary schools: A systemic perspective. *American Journal of Health Education, 52*(5), 251–265. https://doi.org/10.1080/19325037.2021.1955232

Ofsted. (2022). *Early years inspection handbook*. Available via: https://www.gov.uk/government/publications/early-years-inspection-handbook-pdf. Accessed: December 2023.

Ouvry, M. (2003). *Exercising muscles and minds*. London: National Children's Bureau.

Palaiologou, I. (2016). *Child observation* (3rd ed.). London: Sage.

Piaget, J. (1951). *Play, dreams and imitations in childhood*. London: William Heinemann.

Piaget, J. (1953). *The origins of intelligence in the child* (2nd ed.). London: Routledge and Kegan Paul.

Piaget, J. (1959). *The language and thought of the child*. London: Routledge and Kegan Paul.

Piaget, J. (1962). *Play, dreams and imitation in childhood* (2nd ed.). London: Routledge and Kegan Paul.

Piaget, J. (1969). *The mechanisms of perception*. London: Routledge and Kegan Paul.

Piaget, J. (1970). *Science of education and the psychology of the child*. Harlow: Longman.

Piaget, J. (1972). *The principles of genetic epistemology*. London: Routledge and Kegan Paul.

Piaget, J. (1973). *The child and reality: Problems of genetic psychology*. New York: Grossman Publishers.

Piaget, J., & Inhelder, B. (1969). *The psychology of the child: Translated from the French by Helen Weaver*. New York: Basic books.

Pickering, S. (2017). *Teaching outdoors creatively*. London: Routledge.

Play Wales. (2017). *Resources for playing-providing loose parts to support children's play*. Cardiff.

Prince, H., & Cory-Wright, J. (2022). Outdoor education as a deep education for global sustainability and social justice. In K. Petry & J. de Jong (Eds.), *Education in sport & physical activity: Global perspectives & future directions* (pp. 49–59). London: Routledge.

Prince, H. E., & Diggory, O. (2023). Recognition and reporting of outdoor learning in primary schools in England. *Journal of Adventure Education and Outdoor Learning*. https://doi.org/10.1080/14729679.2023.2166544

Prodger, A. (2013). A case study about Jack. In C. Arnold (Ed.), *Mairs K and The Pen Green Team. Young children learning through schemas* (pp. 58–78). London: Routledge.

Rinaldi, C. (2006). *In dialogue with Reggio Emilia: Listening, researching, and learning*. Routledge.

Roe, M. (2007). Feeling 'secrety': Children's views on involvement in landscape decisions. *Environmental Education Research, 13*(4), 467–485.

Sandseter, E. B. H. (2007). Categorizing risky play—How can we identify risk-taking in children's play. *European Early Childhood Education Research Journal, 15*(2), 237–252. Available via: https://www.researchgate.net/publication/249047571_Categorising_risky_play-How_can_we_identify_risk-taking_in_children's_play#fullTextFileContent. Accessed January 2nd 2025.

Sandseter, E. B. H. (2009). Children's expressions of exhilaration and fear in risky play. *Contemporary issues in early childhood, 10*(2), 92–106.

Sandseter, E. B. H., Wyver, S., & Little, H. (2012). Does theory and pedagogy have an impact on provisions for outdoor learning? A comparrison of approaches in Australia and Norway. *Journal of Adventure Education and Outdoor Learning, 12*(3), 167–182.

Schultz, P. W. (2001). The structure of environmental concern: Concern for self, other people, and the biosphere. *Journal of Environmental Psychology, 21*, 327–339.

Singh, A. (2012). Physical activity and performance at school. *Archives of Pediatrics and Adolescent Medicine, 166*(1), Article p49. https://doi.org/10.1001/archpediatrics.2011.716

Sjöblom, P., & Svens, M. (2019). Learning in the Finnish outdoor classroom: Pupils' views. *Journal of Adventure Education and Outdoor Learning, 19*(4), 301–314. https://doi.org/10.1080/14729679.2018.1531042

Smidt, S. (2011). *Playing to learn: The role of play in the early years*. Routledge.

Striniste, N. (2019). *Nature play at home: Creating outdoor spaces that connect children with the natural world*. Portland: Timber Press.

Strong-Wilson, T., & Ellis, J. (2007). Children and place: Reggio Emilia's approach to environmental education. *Children, Youth and Environments, 17*(1), 1–15.

Sturm, B. W. (2008). Imaginary 'geographies' of childhood: School library media centres as secret spaces. *Knowledge Quest, 36*(4), 47–53.

Sunderland, P. (1992). *Cognitive development today: Piaget and his critics*. London: Paul Chapman.

Taguchi, H. L. (2011). Investigating learning participation and becoming in early childhood practices with a relational materialist approach. *Global Studies of Childhood., 1*(1), 36–50.

The Pen Green Schema Group. (2023) *Schemas in the early years*. C. Arnold (Ed.). London, Routledge.

Thomas, A. (2018b). *Planning for schemas in the Welsh curriculum*. Available via: https://hwb.gov.wales/repository/resource/e0ef76fe-334f-45ae-a6c8-7aa630e64310. Accessed 31 October 2023.

Thomas, A. (2018a). *Exploring the role of schemas within the Welsh Foundation Phase curriculum*. Unpublished doctoral dissertation. University of South Wales.

Tovey, H. (2007). *Playing outdoors: Spaces and places, risk and challenge: Spaces and places, risks and challenge*. McGraw-Hill Education.

Tovey, H. (2020). *Froebel's principles and practcie today*. Froebel Trust. Available via: https://froebel.org.uk/training-and-resources/pamphlets. Accessed October 2024.

Vygotsky, L. S. (1978). *Mind in society*. London: Harvard.

WAG. (2009). *Foundation phase outdoor learning handbook*. Cardiff: Crown copyright.

Waite, S. (2010). Losing our way? The downward path for outdoor learning for children aged 2–11 years. *Journal of Adventure Education and Outdoor Learning, 10*(2), 111–126. https://doi.org/10.1080/14729679.2010.531087

Waite, S. (2020). Where are we going? International views on purposes, practices and barriers in school-based outdoor learning. *Education Sciences, 10*(11), 311. https://doi.org/10.3390/educsci10110311

Welsh Government (WG). (2020a). *Curriculum for Wales Guidance*. Crown Copyright.

Welsh Government (WG). (2020b). *Curriculum for Wales*. Available via https://hwb.gov.wales/curriculum-for-wales/designing-your-curriculum/developing-a-vision-for-curriculum-design

Welsh Government (WG). (2022a). *A curriculum for funded non-maintained nursery settings*. Available via: https://hwb.gov.wales/api/storage/b1801d78-38c3-4320-9818-d9996c21aef8/220914-a-curriculum-for-funded-non-maintained-nursery-settings.pdf. Accessed 31 October 2023.

Welsh Government (WG). (2022b). *Schematic development: Noticing and supporting the repeated patterns of behaviour in children's play*. Available via: https://hwb.gov.wales/playlists/view/1d966d4e-a1c7-4b1e-b29f-6090a3a926c7/en/1. Accessed 31 October 2023.

Welsh Government (WG). (2023a). *Observation*. Available via: View—Hwb (gov.wales). Accessed 01 December 2023.

Welsh Government (WG). (2023b). *Early childhood play, learning and care: Developmental pathways 0 to 3*. Available via: https://hwb.gov.wales/api/storage/56774946-48aa-4fab-adda-f27508d8dc8f/early-childhood-play-learning-and-care-developmental-pathways-0-to-3.pdf. Accessed 1st December 2024.
White, J. (2008). *Playing and learning outside. Making provisions for high quality experiences in the outdoor environment*. London: Routledge.
White, J. (2013). *Playing and learning outdoors: Making provision for high quality experiences in the outdoor environment with children 3–7*. Abingdon: Routledge.
White, J. (2023a). *Ecological identity and childhood outdoor play. The outdoor teacher podcasts [Podcast]*. September 25th 2023. Available via: The Wild Minds Podcast | Professor Jan White (theoutdoorteacher.com). Accessed: 26th September 2023.
White, J. (2023b). Feeling at home in the world: Linking schemas with landscape and embodiment understandings. In C. Arnold (Ed.), *Schemas in the early years: Exploring beneath the surface through observation and dialogue* (pp. 137–159). London: Routledge.
Wilenski, D., & Wending, C. (2013). *Ways into Hinchingbrooke country park*. Cambridge: Cambridge Curiosity and Imagination.
Wilson, E. O. (1984). *Biophilia: The human bond with other species*. Cambridge: Harvard University Press.
Wilson, R. (1997). A sense of place. *Early Childhood Education Journal, 24*(3), 191–194.
Wolf, C., Kunz, P., & Robin, N. (2022). Emerging themes of research into outdoor teaching in initial formal teacher training from early childhood to secondary education—A literature review. *The Journal of Environmental Education, 53*(4), 199–220. https://doi.org/10.1080/00958964.2022.2090889
Zelenski, J. M., & Nisbet, E. K. (2012). Happiness and feeling connected: The distinct role of nature relatedness. *Environment and Behaviour, 6*(1). Available via: https://doi.org/10.1177/0013916512451901. Accessed: November 2023.

Index

A
Accommodation, 11
Affordance theory, 1, 6, 7, 40, 46, 47
Arnold, Cath, 3, 5, 15, 16, 57, 87, 91, 121
Assimilation, 11, 12
Atherton, Frances, 3, 16–18, 46, 61, 94, 123
Athey, 2, 5, 11, 13–16, 19, 46, 50, 57, 60, 61, 99, 100, 124, 130, 134
Attuned adult, 19, 59, 94

B
Biophilia, 34

C
Clark, Alison, 27, 30, 32, 33, 35, 49, 50, 94, 114–116, 133, 134, 140, 141
Cognition, 1, 12, 14, 27, 43, 83, 114
Collaboration, 6, 40, 44, 129
Curriculum
   Curriculum for Funded Non-maintained Nursery Settings, 6, 61
   Curriculum for Wales (CfW), 18, 19, 31, 94, 96
   Development Matters, 65
   Early Years Foundation Stage (ESYF), 17, 18
   Realising the Ambition–Being Me, 19
   Reggio Emilia, 33, 129, 130
   Te Whāriki, 17

D
Developmental pathways
   cognitive development, 6, 123
   communication, 18, 64, 79
   exploration, 18, 94, 124
   language development, 83
   physical development, 18, 64, 79, 94, 110, 113
   wellbeing, 61, 79, 94, 110, 124

E
Early Years Foundation Stage (ESYF), 3, 31, 64
Ecological identity, 35, 107
Effective environments, 19, 27, 39, 40, 46, 50, 141
Estyn, 32

F
Forest School, 30, 136
Froebel, 4, 25, 35, 50, 61, 114, 133, 134, 141, 143

G
Gibson, 5, 6, 40, 45, 46, 75, 107, 141

H
Holistic, 27, 30, 32, 50, 139
   development, 4, 34, 35, 39, 40, 45, 46, 69, 140, 142, 143

K
Knowledge and understanding, 1, 2, 5, 7, 11, 27, 36, 46, 52, 59, 60, 80, 96, 98, 100, 113, 140, 143

L

Learning environment, 5, 14, 16, 26, 27, 31, 40, 47, 53, 66, 69, 99, 100, 129, 142
Loose parts, 1, 2, 4, 6, 7, 14, 18, 21, 28, 39–47, 49, 51, 53, 57, 60, 64, 66, 69, 73, 75, 79, 80, 83, 87, 89, 99–101, 105, 110, 118, 119, 121, 123, 124, 130, 134, 135, 139, 141–143
Loose parts play (LPP), 40, 43–45, 50, 60, 80, 98
Louis, Stella, 3, 13, 18, 70, 73, 76, 121

N

Nature connectedness, 34, 35
Nature pedagogy, 34, 36, 50, 115, 118, 130, 136, 140
Neoliberal, 101, 143
  neoliberal clock, 133
Nicholson, Simon, 4, 40, 141
Nutbrown, Cathy, 3, 5, 13, 15, 16, 18, 46, 47, 57, 61, 94, 99, 123, 134, 139, 140, 144

O

Observation, 3, 5, 6, 12, 14–17, 19–22, 31–33, 46, 47, 58, 60, 66, 67, 80, 88, 96, 97, 107, 113, 114, 129–131, 133, 134, 139, 142
Ofsted, 32
Outdoor environments, 1, 4, 25–28, 30, 34–36, 40, 43, 50, 52, 53, 116, 133, 134, 139, 143
Outdoor learning, 1, 2, 4, 5, 7, 25–32, 35, 40, 99, 140
Outdoor pedagogy, 5, 6, 29, 30, 32, 36, 140
Outdoors, 1, 2, 4, 6, 14, 18, 21, 22, 25–32, 35, 36, 39, 40, 42, 44, 46, 49–53, 60, 64, 66, 69, 73, 75, 79, 80, 83, 87, 89–91, 99–101, 107, 113–115, 118, 121, 123, 124, 134, 135, 139–143
Outdoor spaces, 27, 28, 44, 47, 50, 64, 75, 83, 89, 100, 105, 107, 141–143

P

Patterns of play, 118
Pedagogical blindness, 28
Pedagogy, 5, 17, 19, 25, 26, 28–32, 34, 52, 53, 65, 101, 115, 139, 140, 142
Percolate, 27, 33, 35, 47, 50, 94, 105, 115, 133, 134, 140, 141, 144
  percolation of learning, 133

Physical activity, 32, 43, 44, 51
Piaget, 2, 5, 11–16, 27, 58, 60, 61, 83, 109, 117, 140
Piaget, J., 90, 99, 100, 121, 123
Play
  creative play, 42, 133, 134
  outdoor play, 29, 35, 50, 69
  risky play, 6, 51, 124, 141
  transformative play, 53

R

Reflection, 144
Reggio Emilia, 33
Relational materialist lens, 47, 53, 141
Relocating, 105, 118

S

Sandseter, 51, 124
Schemas, 1–3, 5–7, 11–19, 21–23, 27, 31, 33, 42, 45–47, 49–53, 58, 60, 66, 69, 73, 75, 76, 79, 80, 83, 108–110, 113, 114, 117, 139–144
  dynamic schemas, 5, 14, 47, 52, 142
Schema types
  Enclosing, 6
  enclosing, 13, 87, 89, 91–93, 99–101, 130, 141
  enveloping, 6, 13, 18, 49, 51, 87, 88, 90, 94, 95, 99, 100
  orientation, 6, 121, 123–126, 132, 134
  positioning, 6, 14, 21, 121–124, 134, 135
  rotational, 6
  trajectory, 6, 13, 73, 76–80, 82–84, 130
  transporting, 6, 105, 109, 111, 112, 115, 117–119
Self-esteem, 44
Slow knowledge, 32, 35, 115
Slow pedagogy, 30, 32, 94, 100, 101
Social skills, 44, 116, 117
Spaces, 34, 35, 39, 40, 50–53, 75, 79, 80, 83, 88–90, 101, 107–109, 129, 130, 141, 143
  secret spaces, 39, 89, 141
Stage Level Theory, 12
  concrete operational stage, 12
  formal operational stage, 12
  pre-operational stage, 12
  sensori-motor stage, 12

T
Taguchi, 47, 49, 58, 75, 99, 105, 118, 141
Threads of thinking, 3, 13, 15, 47, 99, 100, 140
Time, 2, 7, 13, 16, 21, 27, 31–36, 39, 43, 46, 47, 49, 50, 64, 65, 69, 73, 75, 79, 80, 83, 87, 88, 90, 91, 94, 98, 101, 105, 109, 110, 113–118, 122, 132–134, 140, 142–144

U
Unhurried children, 32, 141

V
Vygotsky, 13–15